BUSINESS ENGLISH 1

RESOURCE BOOK

Sharon Nolan and Bill Reed

Longman

Longman Group UK Limited,
Longman House, Burnt Mill, Harlow,
Essex CM20 2JE, England
and Associated Companies throughout the world.

© Longman Group UK Limited 1992

First published 1992

Set in Ehrhardt and Helvetica

Designed and produced by The Pen and Ink Book Company Ltd,
Huntingdon, Cambridgeshire

Printed in Great Britain by
J. B. Offset Printers (Marks Tey) Ltd, Colchester

ISBN 0582 07843.1

Acknowledgements
The authors would like to thank staff at Western Language
Centre for their support and suggestions during the development
of this material.

Illustrated by Bob Murdoch

CONTENTS

	UNIT	SUGGESTED LANGUAGE FOCUS
	Needs Analysis	Describing job responsibilities
SECTION 1 **The business world**	1 The market	Cause and effect
	2 The future of business	Forecasting
	3 Cultural differences in business	Comparisons and differences
	4 Cultural differences in society	Describing social customs
	5 Demographic trends	Making predictions
	6 The natural environment	Requirements and effects
	7 STEP analysis	Presenting information
SECTION 2 **The organisation**	8 Company structure	Reporting relationships
	9 Company culture	Corporate attitudes
	10 SWOT analysis	Presenting and summarising
	11 Working conditions	Time, days of week, frequency
	12 Managing change	Describing change
	13 Aims and objectives	Stating objectives
	14 The workplace	Location and position
	15 Products and services	Describing products/services
	16 Health and safety	Rules and regulations
SECTION 3 **Doing the job**	17 What do managers do?	Job responsibilities
	18 Demands, choices and constraints	Demands, choices and constraints
	19 Quality	Explaining problems and solutions
	20 Systems	Sequencing
	21 Production processes	Describing processes
	22 Meetings	Stating aims and procedures
	23 Participating in meetings	Describing behaviour
	24 Problem-solving	Hypothesizing, comparing alternatives
	25 Graphs and charts	Presenting visual information
	26 Controlling and monitoring	Cause and effect
	27 Planning	Explaining logistics
SECTION 4 **Working with people**	28 Job advertisements	Job descriptions
	29 Staff selection	Narrating past experience
	30 Communication	Communication systems
	31 Appearance, character, behaviour	Describing people
	32 Working with your boss	Describing values and behaviour
	33 Motivating people	Describing attitudes and responses
	34 People problems	Expressing feelings
	35 Working in a team	Describing teams
	36 Training	Evaluating needs
SECTION 5 **Self-management**	37 Job satisfaction	Expressing opinions
	38 Self assessment	Expressing likes and dislikes
	39 Time management	Expressions of time and proportion
	40 Stress management	Physical and emotional states
	41 Career development	Past, present and future

Elementary	Lower Intermediate	Upper Intermediate	Advanced	PRESENTATION	TIME (minutes)		PAGE
•	•	•	•		45		12
	•	•	•	•	60		15
	•	•	•	•	45		17
	•	•	•		45		19
		•	•		45		20
		•	•		45		22
	•	•	•		60		24
			•	•	60		26
	•	•	•	•	90		28
		•	•		60		30
	•	•	•	•	60	⚠	32
•	•	•	•		45	⚠	33
		•	•		90		35
		•	•		45		37
•	•	•	•		45		38
•		•	•	•	45		40
	•	•	•		45		41
•	•	•	•		45		43
		•	•		45	⚠	45
		•	•	•	60	⚠	46
•	•	•	•		60		48
	•	•	•	•	60		50
	•	•			60		51
			•		60	⚠	53
		•	•	•	90		55
•		•	•	•	60		57
		•	•	•	60		59
	•	•	•	•	90		61
		•	•		45		63
•	•	•	•	•	45	⚠	65
•	•	•	•	•	45		66
•	•				45	⚠	68
		•	•		45	⚠	70
			•		45	⚠	71
			•		60	⚠	73
		•	•		60		74
	•	•	•	•	90		76
		•	•	•	90	⚠	78
		•	•		45	⚠	80
•	•	•	•		45		81
		•	•	•	45	⚠	83
		•	•	•	60	⚠	84

⚠ These units work best with a well-established group in an atmosphere of mutual trust.

INTRODUCTION

WHO IS THIS BOOK FOR?

This book is for teachers of English (or any foreign language) working with business or professional people.

Whatever your own experience we recommend reading this introduction before using any of the units.

WHO CAN IT BE USED WITH?

This book can be used with course participants who are:

- already in work (at whatever level of responsibility)
- business studies students
- in one-to-one or group courses
- in multilingual or monolingual groups
- in language schools or in-company courses
- in the UK or elsewhere
- on intensive or extensive courses
- elementary to advanced level (depending on the unit)

WHY WE WROTE THIS BOOK

Our experience in training language teachers to teach business people has shown us two main areas of concern. The first is the fear of not knowing enough about the business world to be credible in the classroom; the second is the shortage of material which draws directly on the knowledge and experience of course participants and helps teachers to build coherent and meaningful lessons.

A further reason for writing this book is to enable teachers to reveal those areas of language which course participants need and which are not usually identified either by teaching English for communication skills (telephoning, presentations, meetings etc.) or by using course material which predetermines language input. For example, while preparing this book we interviewed a quality control manager in a drinks factory about his work. Central to an explanation of this work were the rates at which products were sampled – every day, at random, one in ten, twice a week, etc. This formed a functional area of language (sampling rates) which this manager needed in order to communicate with others on the job. Only a discussion about his work could have revealed this need.

By using the units in this book you will be able to find out your course participants' job-related language needs.

THE AIMS OF THIS BOOK ARE TO:

- provide an overall framework to help teachers choose themes which motivate course participants.
- give practical lesson plans on these themes which will uncover and exploit the knowledge and experience of course participants.

- create a communicative dynamic in which participants interact on themes which are of direct concern to them.
- allow course participants to be experts in their own field, freeing teachers to be experts in the language field.
- form a continuing process of needs analysis which ensures that participants are taught the language they most need.
- provide structured opportunities for teachers to learn about the business world while focussing on the language needs of course participants.

HOW THIS BOOK WORKS

Participants in business English courses bring with them two valuable resources: personal experience of the world of work and therefore of the contexts in which they will use English; and (unless they are beginners) an ability, however limited, to communicate in English.

This book provides teachers with opportunities to exploit these resources in order to assess language needs and abilities and teach participants the language they most need.

The sections

It is divided into five sections which, together, constitute a framework for understanding, organising and using participants' work experience, regardless of the professional, business or industrial sector they work in. This framework is an overall structure into which the smaller frameworks of the individual units fit. The five sections range from global to individual themes as follows:

 The business world

This is the environment in which all businesses operate. It includes all issues which impinge directly or indirectly on business, whether these issues are sociological, technological, economic, political, legislative or environmental. Because of the scope and implications of these themes, this section also involves the long-term future.

These themes are the concerns of heads of organisations, planners, politicians, people working in research and development, bankers and anyone who is aware that their own work is affected by changes in the outside world.

 The organisation

An organisation is any operational structure: a government, a political party, a multinational corporation, a firm of lawyers, a medical practice, a division or department within a larger organisation, a small family business, a school, or even a family.

Most of your course participants work in one sort of organisation or another. Even business students work within the organisation of a university or business school and most people have lived in a family. All organisations have attitudes, structures, systems and processes which enable them to achieve their objectives. These themes concern all members of organisations in one way or another.

 **Doing the job**

Whereas sections one and two deal with the global and organisational contexts in which people work, section three is concerned with the component tasks of their jobs, and how they are carried out. The themes in this section are designed to be used with participants from a wide variety of jobs.

 **Working with people**

This section deals with human relationships and attitudes at work, whether one-to-one, in a department, in a team or a hierarchy.

 **Self-management**

This section deals with personal assessment, performance and development at work.

Analysing needs

The five sections of the book provide a practical framework for classifying and understanding course participants' work. You can apply it to any job in order to stimulate communication and to discover your participants' main interests. For example, participant X working in, say, personnel, might be concerned with one or more of the following, depending on his or her role in the organisation:

1 The business world: for example, demographic changes likely to affect employment in the future.
2 The organisation: for example, working conditions affecting personnel.
3 Doing the job: for example, recruitment and selection procedures.
4 Working with people: for example, promoting effective team-work.
5 Self management: for example, career development of participant X.

If you have ever thought to yourself 'I know participant Y is an accountant/marketing manager/stockbroker, etc. but what do they actually do?', this framework will be useful to you. This is why we use it in the **Needs Analysis Unit**.

Your first task in analysing needs is to find out which sections of this book are of most use to your course participants. This involves working through the **Needs Analysis Unit**. You may find it useful to read quickly through this unit before going any further.

Once you have completed the **Needs Analysis Unit** and found out which sections of the book are most useful to your course participants, you can choose units within these sections.

The units

Each unit contains a framework designed to reveal course participants' existing language ability, and to highlight gaps and errors. So each unit is a needs analysis in itself, and as the unit themes are different, a variety of language needs will be revealed.

Each unit has the following stages:

1 **An initial task** in preparation for:
2 **A communicative task** where you monitor language ability and needs.
3 **Language feedback, correction and input**; creation of participants' personal language file.
4 **A transfer task** to consolidate language learnt.

In stages 1 and 2 of the unit participants concentrate on the content of the task and on communicating this content to each other, while you monitor them using observation sheets.

In stage 3 they get feedback. You acknowledge accurate language, deal with inaccuracies and give new language input which they note on their personal language file.

In stage 4 they work on a further task in which they use the new or corrected language.

As course participants use their own experience for the content of the task, the language input is relevant to their needs, meaningful and memorable.

Worksheets

Each unit has photocopiable worksheets for course participants to use during the activity and a personal language file to retain for future reference. It may be helpful to use the worksheet layout when writing on the board. It is divided into sections (boxes).

The first box is for participants' individual use during the first stage of the activity, while preparing for the communicative part of the task. This is an essential part of structuring the activity because it gives participants time to think and to organise what they have to say. For this reason box 1 of the worksheet usually contains a skeleton structure, intended to trigger associations and generate and organise individual responses to the theme of the unit. In this way you, as the teacher, do not provide the content at this stage; you ensure that the task and box 1 of the worksheet are understood, giving participants the freedom to provide the content.

Other boxes are developments of the theme of the unit, and form part of individual, pair or group activities.

The personal language file is intended for participants' use during stage 3, the correction and input stage. Each participant therefore individually builds up a dossier of new and corrected language which they need for their work, and which they use in stage 4.

HOW TO TEACH USING THIS BOOK

This section tells you, in detail, how to prepare for teaching, and what to do at each stage. As you become familiar with the book you will also find your own ways of using the material.

Preparing for the activity

At the beginning of each unit we give a guide to the following:

Preparation

This tells you about any items you need to prepare before using the unit. You will always need enough copies of the course participant worksheets, one per person, and a copy of the teacher observation sheets, the first for your initial notes, the second for your classified notes (see *Monitoring the activity* below).

In some cases you may wish to give a piece of authentic material, from a newspaper or magazine, on the same theme, as a follow-up activity.

In order to get a feel for the units and to have some idea of likely language use we recommend working through them yourself as if you were a course participant. For example in Unit 30 (Communication), use your own work context. Most units are applicable to teaching. To find out which ones, do the **Needs Analysis Unit** yourself, or with colleagues.

Time

The time you spend on a unit will depend on the size of the group, the quality and quantity of participant input, the language level and the amount of time you devote to transfer or follow-up activities. As a rough guide times vary between 45 and 90 minutes. The greatest amount of time should be spent on stage 2, the communicative part of the lesson, and stage 3, language feedback, correction and input.

Level

Because there is no prescribed language input for the units in this book there is no optimum level (elementary, intermediate, advanced) required to carry out the tasks in the units.

Ability to carry out the tasks depends on motivation and experience rather than any particular language level. For this reason it is important to select appropriate units (*see* **Needs Analysis Unit**). Naturally the feedback, correction and language input you give will depend upon the level of the participants you are working with.

For each unit we state a range of levels within which it can be used. All units can be used with advanced levels. Some of the tasks require more abstract language and for this reason we have excluded elementary levels.

We have successfully used many of these units with multi-level groups.

Suggested language focus

This is a guide to a language area which participants are likely to need because of the nature of the activity. As the tasks are designed to draw out participants' knowledge and experience in their own words, and as you will base your language feedback, correction and input on their performance of the communicative task, we advise you to make your observation notes before deciding on any language input. This will ensure that your language input corresponds directly to their needs.

You may of course need to supply words and phrases to help the task along in stages 1 and 2. The major language input comes in stage 3 when participants are no longer involved in the task and can concentrate on the language. Do keep notes of words and phrases which you supply in stages 1 and 2, to remind participants later in stage 3.

Facilitating the activity

Initial task

Course participants usually work individually at this stage. You facilitate the process by:

- ensuring that all participants understand the task.
- standing back to observe.
- being available to give individual help if called on.
- noting the points on which you give help.

The most important thing is to get participants actively involved in the task as quickly as possible.

While participants are filling in their worksheets, go round and monitor the activity and what they are writing. This is an opportunity to check words and spelling – an opportunity often lacking in short courses.

Our instructions to you invariably begin:

'Ask participants to . . .'. This assumes that you have already introduced the theme and that participants understand both the theme and your instruction. Sometimes you may wish to take things more gently, by leading up to the task with a few questions of your own.

Some activities begin with a group brainstorming activity.

Monitoring the activity

Communicative task

At this stage course participants work in pairs or groups. While they are interacting, make sure they are not simply reading each other's worksheets, but that they are using them as notes from which to speak to each other. You will probably find that participants are curious to know more about their partner's situation, so this is a good opportunity to check use of question forms, clarifying, checking information, summarising etc.

You monitor the process by:

- noting on the first observation sheet, **Initial observation notes** (see page 86), the actual language used which
  a) is appropriate, accurate, and successful.
  b) leads to misunderstanding.
  c) is clearly wrong.
- classifying items in your observation notes so that you are ready to give constructive, organised feedback. The second observation sheet, **Classified observation notes**, is designed for this purpose (see page 87).

Stage 2 normally ends with pairs or individuals reporting back to the group, which leads to a short discussion. Continue to monitor, using your observation sheet.

How to classify observation notes

As you have had to make notes at speed and in the order in which items occurred, you will now need a few moments to sort them out. Use the **Classified observation notes** sheet on page 87. Do this while participants are rounding off their discussions. Your aim in sorting out these notes will be to present successes, misunderstandings and errors to course participants in an organised way. Your classification will depend on what participants actually said. Look first for any difficulties with the suggested language focus. Although you have not made any previous reference to this, it is likely that participants will have needed this language.

For your other notes look for patterns:

lexical: vocabulary items
structural: grammar structure
functional: discourse functions
phonological: the sounds of the language
conceptual: language expressing concepts needed in the exercise e.g. language of time in the unit on *Time Management*.

The diagrams below give examples of ways in which items in your notes might fit under each heading. This is a guide. You may wish to organise your notes differently. The important thing is to organise them.

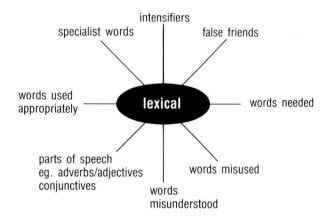

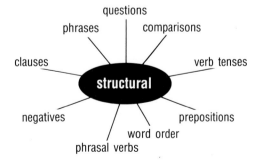

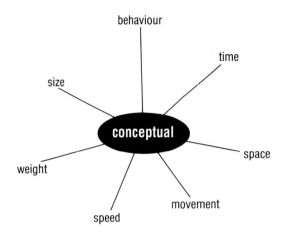

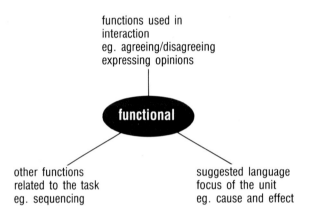

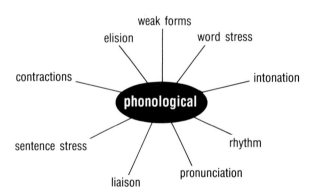

S T A G E

T H R E E Language feedback, correction and input

In this stage of each unit, you give constructive feedback to participants based on your organised notes. The purpose of this is to acknowledge accurate and appropriate language used, to correct mistakes and to present new language.

How to use your observation notes

Firstly acknowledge accurate and appropriate language. These are the items you have written in the left hand column of your classified observation notes. This enables you to:

- acknowledge recent learning.
- highlight good use of language by some individuals from which others can learn.
- use successful language as a springboard to present new language of the same category (function, structure etc.) to extend the participants' range. However, keep major new items for a separate lesson.

Secondly, pick out classes of error from your second column (e.g. structures, phonology etc.). These are your participants' real language needs because they have arisen from a task which draws on their own personal work experience.

Decide which of these needs to work on at this stage, depending on the time available, and which to keep for future lessons.

Participants should write corrections and new language input in their personal language file. **Always check the accuracy and appropriacy of their notes as this is the new and corrected language which participants will be taking away with them.**

Techniques for correction

a) Highlight errors and then encourage participants to correct themselves. Use the following techniques:
  - write one of the participants' incorrect sentences on the board. Say there is something wrong and ask participants to suggest correct versions.
  - write the sentence with a gap in it where a word was misused or missing. Ask them to fill the gap.
  - write up the sentence and give a multiple choice when you come to the incorrect form. Discuss possible correct solutions and their meanings.
  - write up a table of possibilities to form different sentences.
b) Correct items which they are unable to correct themselves. For example, group together phonological items such as minimal pairs or word-stress and give a few minutes' practice.

Techniques for extending participants' language range

a) Take an appropriate language item and ask participants to:
  - suggest other ways of saying the same thing.
  - suggest ways of saying the opposite.
  - make it more formal or informal.
  - make it stronger or weaker.
  - change the timescale (e.g. to work on future or past forms).
b) Present any language which is obviously lacking. It is quite likely that work on the task will have exposed gaps in participants' knowledge which cannot be addressed simply by extending their current range but will need to be dealt with in a separate lesson. Here you will probably want to use your own favourite techniques or course material to present new language in a structured way. However, because the gaps have been exposed in the context of participants' own work, further practice using this context will be meaningful and memorable.

Because the units in this book form a continuing process of needs analysis you can use it to guide yourself and course participants to the parts of your main course material which are most useful to them. This is especially important on short intensive courses where time is at a premium.

Consolidating new language

```
S  T  A  G  E
F  O  U  R
```
Transfer

At this final stage, you present participants with a further task on the theme of the unit. Ask participants to use their personal language file to help them complete the task with accurate and appropriate language.

Ask them to spend a few moments preparing what to say.
During the communicative stage of the transfer activity, when participants are presenting information or speaking to one another, decide whether it is appropriate to interrupt with corrections or to indicate that something is not quite right, or whether to make notes for remedial work later.

If facilities are available, you may wish to make a recording on audio-cassette or video at this stage, for participants to use later, or during self-access sessions.

You can use most transfer activities as follow-up writing exercises for participants who need to practise writing skills.

How to use the presentation preparation sheet

As course participants often need to make presentations at work, the **Transfer** stage of some units includes a short presentation. To help participants prepare for this, give them a copy of the **Presentation preparation sheet** on page 89. It is organised as follows.

- introduction of speaker: to give participants practice in introducing themselves or others.
- theme of presentation: the title or subject.
- main points of presentation: the headings of the topics to be covered.
- parts 1 to 4: for detailed notes on each section (there may be fewer or more parts).
- conclusion: a summary of what has been said, and conclusions drawn.
- questions: a reminder to invite these and allow time for them.

On the right of the sheet, in the column entitled *Language reminders*, participants should write any language notes they will need in the course of the presentation. These might be:

- language focus of the unit
- language needed for presentations: introducing, sequencing, linking, checking understanding, summarising, asking for questions.
- new words or phrases
- pronunciation and stress of key words
- key structures

These can be highlighted for quick reference.

Remarks

In this section of each unit we suggest alternative classroom strategies and in some cases give checklists for your own background information, to help you develop the theme of the unit. We refer to source material in this section where appropriate.

One-to-one

For consistency, we have written all units with groups in mind. In our experience all the units work equally well with individuals. The one-to-one section contains notes on the adjustments you need to make to the dynamic of the activity when teaching an individual.

These adjustments will mean that you often have to work as the other half of a pair with your participant, asking questions, clarifying and receiving information. As you will therefore be involved in the content of the activity, you will find it more difficult to stand back and make language notes. For this reason we recommend that you record these exchanges on audio-cassette so that you can separate the work on the language from the work on the task. By playing back the cassette you can involve your participant in the process of language analysis and correction, thus encouraging self-assessment.

When you participate in the activity, you need to use your own work experience. We recommend that, if possible, you take your examples from past jobs so as to distance yourself from your present situation. This is to avoid discussion which could be embarrassing to you or to your organisation.

In order to exploit the unit theme fully in one-to-one, you may wish to give out the worksheet beforehand so that your participant can prepare in as much detail as possible.

Groups

Individual responses to the task will often be of interest to other members of the group. Exploit this situation fully: it is a natural information gap. Be aware of cross-cultural, inter-organisational and inter-departmental differences which arise, so that you can use this dynamic in the group.

Needs analysis. What do you do?

INTRODUCTION

This unit analyses needs in two ways:

1) by highlighting business and work themes which are of direct concern to course participants.
2) by giving you an initial opportunity to assess participants' existing language ability, and diagnose major language needs.

After using this unit you will be able to chart a path through this book by selecting the sections and units which are of most use to course participants. You can do this by analysing participants' completed worksheets and finding related themes on the Contents page.

The language needs analysis you make using this unit is only the beginning of a continuing process. Each unit in this book has an important diagnostic aspect which enables you to continue analysing and meeting language needs.

This unit follows the same pattern as the other units in the book. Please read the section *How to teach using this book*.

LEVEL Elementary to advanced   TIME 45 minutes

SUGGESTED LANGUAGE FOCUS

Participants' job responsibilities   When making your observation notes, listen in particular for language of job responsibilities which participants:
a) express well.
b) express inaccurately.
c) need to learn in order to communicate their ideas.

PREPARATION

A copy of the worksheet and personal language file for each participant.
A copy of the observation sheets for yourself.

Initial task

- Explain to participants that this activity will enable you to:

    a) identify business and work-related themes of direct concern to them.
    b) assess their language ability and needs.

- Hand out a worksheet to each participant. Ask them to fill in box 1 with a list of the main tasks they have in their jobs. Elementary level participants will need some help from you. Ask for a list of five to ten items, each beginning with a verb. If participants produce a list which is too short or too broad, ask them to give a breakdown of component tasks. For example, the task 'sell product A' might break down into:

    research the market.
    communicate with the marketing department.
    set sales targets.
    motivate the sales force.
    organise myself to do these things.

- Once they have completed their notes, ask each individual to put their list on the board. Alternatively, you write their items on the board as they dictate them to you. There is no need to keep any particular order; you could, for example, ask for one item at a time from each participant in a group.

- At very low levels answers will probably be incomplete. In certain circumstances it may be possible to do the exercise in the native language of the course participant.

Communicative task

STAGE TWO 2

- Divide participants into small groups and ask them to classify the items on the board under the headings in box 2 of their worksheet (see page 2 of the Introduction for clarification of these headings). For example, the items above for selling 'Product A' fit under headings 1 to 5 respectively. While they are discussing this, give help where required and make notes on your observation sheet of the language they use and the language they need (see the section **How to teach using this book**). These notes form your initial language needs analysis for the group or individual. If you have a large group to assess, it is useful to involve another teacher or split the group and deal with one sub-group at a time while the others are engaged in a different activity.

- Note the items listed on the board, and notice any particular items which provoke interest and discussion within the group. These are likely to be useful topics for future lessons. Two participants with completely different jobs may find that they both have an interest in, say, quality.

- End this stage with a group discussion on the items they have included under each heading. This is an opportunity to ask individuals to give examples and justify their choices, and a chance for you to begin to gauge which sections of this book will be of most use to you in planning their course.

Language feedback

STAGE THREE 3

- This unit is designed as an initial assessment of language needs and as a guide to topics of interest to participants. You will need time to read your notes, reflect and prepare a course plan. Feedback in the form of correction and language input in this needs analysis unit will not play as large a part as it does in the other units of this book.

- However, you may already have found some major areas which need to be included in the course and want to mention these to course participants now. Otherwise the major feedback from this unit will come when you present the course plan you have prepared, showing how units from this book will be used in relation to your other course material.

Transfer

- Ask participants to choose an item from their initial list of tasks on their worksheet box 1.
- Ask them to explain, either in pairs or in the group, how they perform this task.

REMARKS

We have assumed in this needs analysis that you are starting out with a new group or an individual. If you have an individual joining an existing group ask them to complete the worksheet in their own time and to explain it briefly to you, or to the whole group, when you next meet.

Because communication plays a central role in people's work, Unit 30 (Communication) can be used as a complement to the initial needs analysis. It can also help in identifying the situations in which course participants need to use English.

ONE-TO-ONE

1 Follow the same procedure, omitting pair or group work and using the worksheet as a framework for discussion with your course participant.
2 Record your conversation on audio-cassette for you and your course participant to analyse later.
3 Any other teacher working with the same course participant should listen to it to get information on language ability and work responsibilities to avoid unnecessary duplication of classroom work.

1 The market

LEVEL   Lower intermediate to advanced   TIME   1 hour

SUGGESTED LANGUAGE FOCUS

Cause and effect   When making your observation notes, listen in particular for language of cause and effect which participants:
a) express well.
b) express inaccurately.
c) need to learn in order to communicate their ideas.

PREPARATION

A copy of the worksheet and personal language file for each participant.
A copy of the presentation preparation sheet for each participant.
A copy of the observation sheets for yourself.

 **Initial task**

In stages 1 and 2, help with language to facilitate the task where necessary.

- Ask participants to write their product or service at the top of the worksheet, or to choose one from the range their company produces, and indicate whether it is sold to individual consumers or to businesses.
- Ask participants to tick the words in the check-list in box 2 which best correspond to the state of the market for their product or service giving a reason to illustrate each tick.

 **Communicative task**

During this stage monitor the discussions and make language notes on the observation sheet (see page 86).

- Ask participants to exchange information in pairs.
- Ask each participant to select one of the words they have ticked from the list in worksheet box 2 and to explain briefly to the group the reason they have written down.
- Ask participants, in pairs, to help each other brainstorm factors which influence customers in the market for their respective product or service, using box 3 of the worksheet. The question is: What makes people buy, or resist buying, this product or service?'
- Ask individuals to explain to the group their notes in box 3.

 **Language feedback**

- Classify your observation notes (see page 7).
- Acknowledge accurate and appropriate language in the left-hand section of your observation sheet (see page 7).
- Pick out classes of error and work on these with participants. See page 9 for techniques of correction and extending language range.
- Present new language which is needed (see page 9).
- Ask participants to write new and corrected language in their personal language files under the headings *Cause and Effect* and *Other language notes*. These are for use during the *Transfer* stage, and to keep for future reference.

 **Transfer**

- Ask participants to use their worksheet and personal language file, and the presentation preparation sheet to prepare a brief presentation on the past, present or future state of the market for their product or service.

If working with an in-company group you have the options of asking them to talk about their own products or services, or about products and services which they are familiar with from other jobs, or about products and services which they use.

An alternative initial task is to brainstorm consumer products or services which participants have used in the past 24 hours (do this on the board). Ask participants to form small groups; each group chooses one item from the board and writes it in box 1. Then proceed as above.

O N E - T O - O N E

1 Follow the same procedure, omitting pair or group work and using the worksheet as a framework for discussion with your course participant.
2 Record your conversation on audio-cassette for you and your course participant to analyse later.

2 The future of business

LEVEL Lower intermediate to advanced   **TIME** 45 minutes

S U G G E S T E D L A N G U A G E F O C U S

Forecasting When making your observation notes, listen in particular for language of forecasting which participants:
a) express well.
b) express inaccurately.
c) need to learn in order to communicate their ideas.

P R E P A R A T I O N

A copy of the worksheet and personal language file for each participant.
A copy of the presentation preparation sheet for each participant.
A copy of the observation sheets for yourself.
Get copies of a short, up to date newspaper or magazine article on the future of business for optional use in the *Transfer* stage.

Initial task

In stages 1 and 2, help with language to facilitate the task where necessary.

- Ask participants to think of three words each, which describe how they would like business in their country to be in the future.
- Ask them to write these words on the left of their worksheet, and to be prepared to explain their choice.
- Ask them to tell you the words. Write them on the left of the board, while asking for explanation and clarification.

STAGE TWO — Communicative task

During this stage monitor the discussions and make language notes on the observation sheet (see page 86).

- Divide participants into small groups to discuss what businesses will need to do to realise these objectives. Ask them to write down necessary action on the right hand side of the worksheet.
- Ask a representative from each group to write up on the right of the board the outcome of the discussion, and to give explanations.
- Ask each participant to make a sentence linking ideas on the left and right of the board giving a timescale in the future.

STAGE THREE — Language feedback

- Classify your observation notes (see page 7).
- Acknowledge accurate and appropriate language in the left hand section of your observation sheet (see page 7).
- Pick out classes of error and work on these with participants. See page 9 for techniques of correction and extending language range.
- Present new language which is needed (see page 9).
- Ask participants to write new and corrected language in their personal language files under the headings *Forecasting* and *Other language notes*. These are for use during the *Transfer* stage, and to keep for future reference.

STAGE FOUR — Transfer

- Ask participants to use their worksheet and personal language file, and the presentation preparation sheet, as a basis for a short presentation on the future of their business.
- Distribute copies of the article dealing with issues affecting the future of business.
- Discuss with participants how the themes in the article relate to the ones they have already discussed.

REMARKS

Individual participants will probably have their own approach. Ideas which may come up in stage 1 are nouns such as: *quality, profitability, new technology, creativity.*

Action needed to achieve these objectives (stage 2) might be verbs such as: *create (quality circles), develop (new marketing strategies), invest, train.*
An example of a link between two ideas is: 'We aim to improve quality through the creation of quality circles.'

ONE-TO-ONE

1 Follow the same procedure, omitting pair or group work and using the worksheet as a framework for discussion with your course participant.
2 Record your conversation on audio-cassette for you and your course participant to analyse later.

3 Cultural differences in business

L E V E L   Lower intermediate to advanced   T I M E   45 minutes

S U G G E S T E D   L A N G U A G E   F O C U S

Making comparisons and expressing differences   When making your observation
notes, listen in particular for language of comparison and difference which participants:
a) express well.
b) express inaccurately.
c) need to learn in order to communicate their ideas.

P R E P A R A T I O N

A copy of the worksheet and personal language file for each participant.
A copy of the observation sheets for yourself.

Initial task

In stages 1 and 2, help with language to facilitate the task where necessary.

- Ask participants to mark in box 1 of their worksheet any point(s) on the list which they
  have experienced as different when doing business in other countries.
- Next ask them to write how they noticed the difference and how it affected their work,
  filling in box 1.

Communicative task

*During this stage monitor the discussions and make language notes on the observation sheet
(see page 86).*

- Ask participants to explain their notes to a partner. Ask pairs to tell the group what
  differences they found when they compared notes.
- Ask participants in what ways they feel awareness of other cultures helps them to do
  business successfully.

Language feedback

- Classify your observation notes (see page 7).
- Acknowledge accurate and appropriate language in the left hand section of your
  observation sheet (see page 7).
- Pick out classes of error and work on these with participants. See page 9 for techniques of
  correction and extending language range.
- Present new language which is needed (see page 9).
- Ask participants to write new and corrected language in their personal language files
  under the headings *Making comparisons*, *expressing differences* and *Other language
  notes*. These are for use during the *Transfer* stage, and to keep for future reference.

Transfer

- Ask individuals to fill in worksheet box 2 using the items in box 1 as a checklist, if necessary. If there are several people of the same nationality in the group, they can get together to do this.

- Ask participants to use their worksheet and personal language file to discuss worksheet box 2 as a group.

REMARKS

With a multilingual group try to seat participants so that pairs will be of different nationalities.

If you wish to alter or extend worksheet box 1 here are some other items:

protocol	equal opportunities
social contacts	bribes
trade fairs	counting, numbers, dates etc.
time management	signs and symbols
presentations	the law

ONE-TO-ONE

1 Follow the same procedure, omitting pair or group work and using the worksheet as a framework for discussion with your course participant.
2 Record your conversation on audio-cassette for you and your course participant to analyse later.

Cultural differences in society

LEVEL Upper intermediate to advanced   TIME 45 minutes

SUGGESTED LANGUAGE FOCUS:

Describing social customs When making your observation notes, listen in particular for language describing social customs which participants:
a) express well.
b) express inaccurately.
c) need to learn in order to communicate their ideas.

PREPARATION

A copy of the worksheet and personal language file for each participant.
A copy of the observation sheets for yourself.

Initial task

In stages 1 and 2, help with language to facilitate the task where necessary.

- Ask participants to tell you the most striking difference between customs in their own country and in the foreign country they have most recently visited. Write these in note form on the board as examples illustrating the theme.
- Ask participants to mark in box 1 of their worksheet any point on the list which they have experienced as different when visiting another country.
- Next ask them to write how it was different and what they had expected, filling in box 1.

Communicative task

During this stage monitor the discussions and make language notes on the observation sheet (see page 86).

- Ask participants to explain their notes to a partner. Ask the listeners to note down a couple of examples of what they are told, in order to tell the group later.
- Ask participants to tell their partner's story to the group.

Language feedback

- Classify your observation notes (see page 7).
- Acknowledge accurate and appropriate language in the left hand section of your observation sheet (see page 7).
- Pick out classes of error and work on these with participants. See page 9 for techniques of correction and extending language range.
- Present new language which is needed (see page 9).
- Ask participants to write new and corrected language in their personal language files under the headings *Describing social customs* and *Other language notes*. These are for use during the *Transfer* stage, and to keep for future reference.

Transfer

Ask individuals to fill in worksheet box 2 using the checklist in box 1, if necessary. If there are several people of the same nationality in the group they can get together to do this.
Ask participants to use their worksheet and personal language file to discuss worksheet box 2 as a group.

REMARKS

Note that *Cultural differences in society* is aimed at a higher level of language ability than *Cultural differences in business*. If you don't want to tackle the past perfect or reported speech, use the procedure in *Cultural differences in business* and alter the question 'What had you expected?' to 'What was your reaction?'

If you wish to alter or extend the worksheet questionnaire, here are some possible themes: *censorship, table etiquette, ethnic stereotypes, titles and forms of address, status symbols, public holidays, courtesy, the family, gifts: giving and receiving, seating arrangements.*

ONE-TO-ONE

1 Follow the same procedure, omitting pair or group work and using the worksheet as a framework for discussion with your course participant.
2 Record your conversation on audio-cassette for you and your course participant to analyse later.

5 Demographic trends

LEVEL Upper intermediate to advanced   TIME 45 minutes

SUGGESTED LANGUAGE FOCUS

Making predictions When making your observation notes, listen in particular for language of predictions which participants:
a) express well.
b) express inaccurately.
c) need to learn in order to communicate their ideas.

PREPARATION

A copy of the worksheet and personal language file for each participant.
A copy of the observation sheets for yourself.

STAGE ONE **Initial task**

In stages 1 and 2, help with language to facilitate the task where necessary.

• Ask participants to fill in the questionnaire in worksheet box 1 saying whether each item is rising or falling in their own country. Space is left for extra items if they wish to add any. Accurate statistical answers are not necessary. Participants' own impressions will be enough. They do not have to answer every question.

STAGE TWO **Communicative task**

During this stage monitor the discussions and make language notes on the observation sheet (see page 86).

• Ask participants to exchange information in pairs.
• Ask them which items from the list in worksheet box 1 affect the workforce in their organisation. What is the present situation and how is it likely to evolve? Ask them to fill in worksheet box 2.
• Discuss as a group and identify any common trends.

Language feedback

- Classify your observation notes (see page 7).
- Acknowledge accurate and appropriate language in the left hand section of your observation sheet (see page 7).
- Pick out classes of error and work on these with participants. See page 9 for techniques of correction and extending language range.
- Present new language which is needed (see page 9).
- Ask participants to write new and corrected language in their personal language files under the headings *Making predictions* and *Other language notes*. These are for use during the *Transfer* stage, and to keep for future reference.

Transfer

- Ask participants to fill in worksheet box 3 with the demographic factors from box 1 which will affect the market for their organisation's products or services in the future.
  For example, the ageing population in Europe will require greater health care provision and leisure opportunities in the next century. Ask participants to use their worksheet and personal language file for further group discussion. Ask the group to agree on some common trends which are likely to affect them all.

R E M A R K S

Keep your eye open for relevant articles in the press to use either as an introduction or a follow-up.

O N E - T O - O N E

1 Follow the same procedure, omitting pair or group work and using the worksheet as a framework for discussion with your course participant.
2 Record your conversation on audio-cassette for you and your course participant to analyse later.

6 The natural environment

LEVEL Lower intermediate to advanced   **TIME** 1 hour

SUGGESTED LANGUAGE FOCUS

Describing requirements and effects When making your observation notes, listen in
particular for language of requirements and effects which participants:
a) express well.
b) express inaccurately.
c) need to learn in order to communicate their ideas.

PREPARATION
A copy of the worksheet and personal language file for each participant.
A copy of the observation sheets for yourself.

 **Initial task**

In stages 1 and 2, help with language to facilitate the task where necessary.

- Ask participants to tell you what the natural environment consists of (see *Remarks*). Write
  their answers on the board.
- Divide participants into small groups and ask them to classify the answers under headings
  of their own choice. Reunite and compare headings.
- Ask participants to fill in the worksheet individually, for their own organisation, noting both
  what they need *from* the environment and any effects *on* the environment following the
  steps given:

  1 Resources and raw materials used
  2 The geographical location of the organisation
  3 The processes and co-ordination required
  4 The products and services supplied
  5 Long-term considerations

 **Communicative task**

*During this stage monitor the discussions and make language notes on the observation sheet
(see page 86).*

- Ask participants to explain their worksheets to each other in pairs.
- Participants now exchange worksheets so that each is in possession of the other's.
  Designate partners A and B, and form a group of As and a group of Bs. Each group will
  therefore have information on the other group's organisations. Ask participants to present
  their partner's worksheet to the group; and ask the group to recommend appropriate
  company policy on the environment in each case.

Language feedback

- Classify your observation notes (see page 7).
- Acknowledge accurate and appropriate language in the left hand section of your observation sheet (see page 7).
- Pick out classes of error and work on these with participants. See page 9 for techniques of correction and extending language range.
- Present new language which is needed (see page 9).
- Ask participants to write new and corrected language in their personal language files under the headings, *Describing requirements and effects* and *Other language notes*. These are for use during the *Transfer* stage, and to keep for future reference.

Transfer

- Ask participants to use their worksheet and personal language file to present their findings to each other, commenting on the appropriacy and feasibility of the proposal made.

R E M A R K S

At stage 1 the classifications could be:
Earth – animal, *mineral*, *vegetable*.
Air – atmosphere, *gases*, *movement*, *climate*.
Water – rivers, *lakes*, *seas*.

In stage 2, if you have a large group, an alternative is to make two group As and two group Bs; or to limit the choice of themes.

O N E - T O - O N E

In stage 2, help your participant formulate an appropriate company policy. In the *Transfer* stage, ask him or her to present this policy briefly and record it on audio-cassette or video (see notes page 11).

7 STEP analysis

L E V E L   Advanced   T I M E   1 hour

S U G G E S T E D   L A N G U A G E   F O C U S

Presenting information   When making your observation notes, listen in particular for language of presenting information which participants:
a) express well.
b) express inaccurately.
c) need to learn in order to communicate their ideas.

P R E P A R A T I O N

A copy of the worksheet and personal language file for each participant.
A copy of the observation sheets for yourself.
A copy of the presentation preparation sheet for each participant.

 **STAGE ONE** **Initial task**

In stages 1 and 2, help with language to facilitate the task where necessary.

- Explain to participants that you are going to ask them to think of their organisation in relation to the world around it, and give their partners information from which to make short presentations.
- Ask participants to write in box 1 of their worksheet two examples of each of the following as they affect their organisations:

  Sociological factors
  Technological factors
  Economic factors
  Political factors

  See *Remarks* for examples.

 **STAGE TWO** **Communicative task**

During this stage monitor the discussions and make language notes on the observation sheet (see page 86).

- Ask participants to interview each other in pairs to obtain as much detail as possible about how each factor affects their partner's organisation, and fill in worksheet box 2.
- Distribute copies of the presentation preparation sheet and ask participants to help each other to prepare presentations based on worksheet box 2.

Language feedback

- Classify your observation notes (see page 7).
- Acknowledge accurate and appropriate language in the left hand section of your observation sheet (see page 7).
- Pick out classes of error and work on these with participants. See page 9 for techniques of correction and extending language range.
- Present new language which is needed (see page 9).
- Ask participants to write new and corrected language in their personal language files under the headings *Presenting information* and *Other language notes*. These are for use during the *Transfer* stage and to keep for future reference.

Transfer

Ask participants to use their worksheet and personal language file, and the presentation preparation sheet, to make short presentations based on the information they have gathered from their partners.

R E M A R K S

The STEP framework is a means of analysing the factors affecting organisations or industries under the following four headings:

Sociological factors
(*Cultural attitudes, language, social attitudes, average age of population, education, industrial relations etc.*)

Technological factors
(*Know-how, computerisation, automation, communications systems, transport etc.*)

Economic factors
(*Inflation, recession, exchange rates, interest rates, monetary systems etc.*)

Political factors
(*Government policy, legislation, international relations, war etc.*)

It can be applied to virtually any theme which involves the interaction of a specific organisation or industry and the world at large. It is useful in understanding and interpreting press articles, news items, case studies, etc. Some factors may fit under more than one heading, depending on the light in which they are viewed. For example, quotas in the motor industry are both political and economic.

Many participants have to use the language in a social context, and their ability to talk in general terms about the business climate is often central to their English language needs.

O N E - T O - O N E

Concentrate on your participant's organisation. Ask your participant to fill in box 1 of the worksheet. Discuss this with him or her and record on audio-cassette. Give language feedback, correction and input and help your participant to prepare a presentation. Record this on video
if facilities are available.

8 Company structure

L E V E L   Lower intermediate to advanced   **T I M E**   1½ hours

SUGGESTED LANGUAGE FOCUS

Reporting relationships   When making your observation notes, listen in particular for language of reporting relationships which participants:
a) express well.
b) express inaccurately.
c) need to learn in order to communicate their ideas.

PREPARATION

A copy of the worksheet and personal language file for each participant.
A copy of the observation sheets for yourself.
A copy of the presentation preparation sheet for each participant.

STAGE ONE   Initial task

In stages 1 and 2, help with language to facilitate the task where necessary.

- Ask participants to draw a diagram in box 1 of the worksheet showing their reporting relationships at work. Tell them there are two ways in which they can do this:
  1) present a formal organigram of their company or department, as for example a box diagram.
  2) present a personal view of the organisation showing who reports to them, and to whom they report, and for what. This could be a spider diagram.
- Ask participants to fill in box 2 of the worksheet.

28

Communicative task

STAGE
T W O
2

During this stage monitor the discussions and make language notes on the observation sheet (see page 86).

- Ask participants to discuss each point from box 2 with a partner.
- Distribute copies of the presentation preparation sheet (see page 89) and ask the pairs to help each other to prepare a simple presentation (3–5 minutes) explaining the structure of their company or department, using the sheet to help them structure their work.
- Ask participants to rehearse their presentation with each other, keeping strict timing.

Language feedback

STAGE
T H R E E
3

- Classify your observation notes (see page 7).
- Acknowledge accurate and appropriate language in the left hand section of your observation sheet (see page 7).
- Pick out classes of error and work on these with participants. See page 9 for techniques for correction and extending language range.
- Present new language which is needed (see page 9).
- Ask participants to write new and corrected language in their personal language files under the headings, *Reporting relationships* and *Other language notes*. These are for use during the *Transfer* stage and to keep for future reference.

Transfer

STAGE
F O U R
4

- Ask participants to use their worksheet and personal language file to finalise and give their presentations. If facilities are available, record these on video for participants to watch later. Ask participants who are listening to prepare questions to ask at the end.

R E M A R K S

For your own background information you may wish to read the section on company structure in Charles Handy's *Understanding Organisations*, chapter 5 (see bibliography). If you have a large group it may be more practical to have presentations on different days to avoid overload.

O N E - T O - O N E

1 Follow the same procedure, omitting pair or group work and using the worksheet as a framework for discussion with your course participant.
2 Record your conversation on audio-cassette for you and your course participant to analyse later.

9 Company culture

L E V E L   Upper intermediate to advanced   T I M E   1 hour

S U G G E S T E D   L A N G U A G E   F O C U S

Corporate attitudes   When making your observation notes, listen in particular for language of corporate attitudes which participants:
a) express well.
b) express inaccurately.
c) need to learn in order to communicate their ideas.

P R E P A R A T I O N

A copy of the worksheet and personal language file for each participant.
A copy of the observation sheets for yourself.

1 STAGE ONE   Initial task

In stages 1 and 2, help with language to facilitate the task where necessary.

- Ask participants to define in a few words how their company is viewed by its customers and the outside world. Write the key words on the board.
- Ask participants to think now of how their company looks to them, from the inside, and to answer the questions about their workplace on the worksheet. Ask them to give examples where they can, and be ready to explain their examples.
- Participants can focus on the areas they perceive as significant. Tell them they do not have to answer all the questions.

2 STAGE TWO   Communicative task

During this stage monitor the discussions and make language notes on the observation sheet (see page 86).

- Ask participants to work in pairs and explain their worksheet to their partner, saying why they chose their topics, why their remarks are significant, and noting down the differences in culture between their organisations.
- Ask participants to report to the group on the similarities and differences they found during the pairwork.

3 STAGE THREE   Language feedback

- Classify your observation notes (see page 7).
- Acknowledge accurate and appropriate language in the left hand section of your observation sheet (see page 7).
- Pick out classes of error from the second section of your observation sheet and work on these with participants. See page 9 for techniques of correction and extending language range.

- Present new language which is needed (see page 9).
- Ask participants to write new and corrected language in their personal language files under the headings *Describing corporate attitudes* and *Other language notes*. These are for use during the *Transfer* stage and to keep for future reference.

Transfer

- Ask participants to use their worksheet and personal language file to compare the cultures of two different parts of their organisation, and to present their observations to the group for discussion. See the *Remarks* section for ways to develop this discussion.

R E M A R K S

A company's culture is related to its structure, so the check-list given in worksheet 4 of the previous unit can be used to extend discussion. Culture can also be affected by the stage of development of an organisation.
Relevant questions are:

Is the organisation facing a crisis?
Is it just setting up, or innovating?
Is it stable and unchanging?
Is it in decline?

Within a company there may well be different cultures in operation at different levels or in different sections. For example, R & D may appear informal, or observe their own time schedules, whereas accounts may dress conservatively and observe strict office hours. Further discussion can focus on the appropriacy of different cultures for different circumstances.
Other questions are:

Do your competitors have a similar culture?
Did your last company have a similar culture?
Are there any culture clashes within your company?
Is the existing culture right for your company or department?

It could be interesting to compare the cultures of two different types of organisation, for example a company and a university, or a family and an army.

O N E - T O - O N E

1 Follow the same procedure, omitting pair or group work and using the worksheet as a framework for discussion with your course participant.
2 Record your conversation on audio-cassette for you and your course participant to analyse later.

10 SWOT analysis

L E V E L Lower intermediate to advanced   T I M E 1 hour

S U G G E S T E D L A N G U A G E F O C U S

Presenting and summarising When making your observation notes, listen in particular for language of presenting and summarising which participants:
a) express well.
b) express inaccurately.
c) need to learn in order to communicate their ideas.

P R E P A R A T I O N

A copy of the worksheet and personal language file for each participant.
A copy of the observation sheets for yourself.
A copy of the presentation preparation sheet for each participant.

STAGE ONE Initial task

In stages 1 and 2, help with language to facilitate the task where necessary.

- Ask participants to write in box 1 of their worksheet two examples of each of the following for their own organisation:

  Strengths inside the organisation
  Weaknesses inside the organisation
  Opportunities which the organisation could use to its advantage
  Threats which could be damaging to the organisation

STAGE TWO Communicative task

During this stage monitor the discussions and make language notes on the observation sheet (see page 86).

- Ask participants to work with a partner and to obtain as much detail as possible about how each factor affects their partner's organisation and to fill in worksheet box 2.
- Distribute copies of the presentation preparation sheet and ask participants to help each other to prepare presentations based on worksheet box 2.

STAGE THREE Language feedback

- Classify your observation notes (see page 7).
- Acknowledge accurate and appropriate language in the left hand section of your observation sheet (see page 7).
- Pick out classes of error and work on these with participants. See page 9 for techniques of correction and extending language range.
- Present new language which is needed (see page 9).

- Ask participants to write new and corrected language in their personal language files under the headings *Presenting and Summarising* and *Other language notes*. These are for use during the *Transfer* stage and to keep for future reference.

Transfer

- Ask participants to use their worksheet and personal language file to make short presentations based either on their own organisation, or on their partner's organisation. Ask listeners to prepare questions to ask at the end of each presentation.

REMARKS

The SWOT framework is used to analyse the factors affecting an organisation at any particular point in time. The internal factors are classified as the organisation's intrinsic *Strengths* and *Weaknesses*; the external factors are the *Opportunities* which the organisation may be able to take advantage of and the *Threats* facing the organisation from outside. Thus, for example, inadequate quality control constitutes a *Weakness*, while the rise of a new competitor is a *Threat*.

The procedure given here serves to introduce the SWOT concepts. A useful application in teaching is in understanding and interpreting case studies and news items and in contributing to a decision making process. It can often be used in conjunction with the STEP framework (see Unit 7).

ONE-TO-ONE

Concentrate on your participant's organisation. Ask your participant to fill in box 1 of the worksheet. Discuss this with them and record on audio-cassette. Give language feedback, correction and input and help your participant to prepare a presentation. Record this on video if facilities are available.

11 Working conditions

LEVEL Elementary to advanced   TIME 45 minutes

SUGGESTED LANGUAGE FOCUS

Time, days of the week and frequency   When making your observation notes, listen in particular for language of time, days of the week and frequency which participants:
a) express well.
b) express inaccurately.
c) need to learn in order to communicate their ideas.

PREPARATION

A copy of the worksheet and personal language file for each participant.
A copy of the observation sheets for yourself.

Initial task

In stages 1 and 2, help with language to facilitate the task where necessary.

- Ask participants to fill in box 1 of the worksheet, stating their own usual working conditions.

Communicative task

During this stage monitor the discussions and make language notes on the observation sheet (see page 86).

- Ask participants to compare notes and discuss in pairs.
- Ask pairs to report back to the group and discuss.

Language feedback

- Classify your observation notes (see page 7).
- Acknowledge accurate and appropriate language in the left hand section of your observation sheet (see page 7).
- Pick out classes of error and work on these with participants. See page 9 for techniques of correction and extending language range.
- Present new language which is needed (see page 9).
- Ask participants to write new and corrected language in their personal language files under the headings *Time, days of the week, frequency* and *Other language notes*. These are for use during the *Transfer* stage and to keep for future reference.

Transfer

- Ask participants to use their worksheet and personal language file to discuss in the group how and why working conditions have changed over the years in different countries or companies.

REMARKS

This is a good ice-breaking activity at the beginning of a course. There is a natural information gap between different nationalities or organisations. You can also compare past and present jobs. However, if your participants work in the same organisation, the success of this unit will depend on the degree of trust within the group.

ONE-TO-ONE

1 Follow the same procedure, omitting pair or group work and using the worksheet as a framework for discussion with your course participant.
2 Record your conversation on audio-cassette for you, and your course participant to analyse later.

If you want to extend the discussion, ask your participant to compare working conditions in present and past jobs.

12 Managing change

L E V E L   Upper intermediate to advanced   T I M E   1½ hours

S U G G E S T E D   L A N G U A G E   F O C U S

Describing change   When making your observation notes, listen in particular for language describing change which participants:
a) express well.
b) express inaccurately.
c) need to learn in order to communicate their ideas.

P R E P A R A T I O N

A copy of the worksheet and personal language file for each participant.
A copy of the presentation preparation sheet for each participant.
A copy of the observation sheets for yourself.

Initial task

- In stages 1 and 2, help with language to facilitate the task where necessary.
- In box 1 of the worksheet ask participants to write a few words about an aspect of their work which they would like to change.

Communicative task

During this stage monitor the discussions and make language notes on the observation sheet (see page 86).

- Ask participants to exchange their information in pairs. As they do this, go round the group listening, and pick out one participant whose change seems appropriate for general discussion.
- Ask this person for permission to discuss the change as an example for the group. Draw a rectangle in the centre of the board, as in box 2 of the worksheet, and ask a few questions of the group member to determine, in a nutshell, what the desired result of the change is. Write this in a few words in the rectangle. Now interview the participant yourself to find out what factors will help achieve the desired result (note these on the board below the rectangle); and what factors will obstruct achievement of the desired result (note them above the rectangle). Factors helping or obstructing achievement of the desired result may be: *people, equipment, money, time, space.* Open the discussion to the group for suggested additions and questions. When you have a reasonably complete picture on the board, ask the participant which of the factors (helping or obstructing) can be influenced, in practice, to achieve the desired result, which obstructing factors can be reduced and which helping factors can be reinforced. Finally, ask the group whether they think the desired result can be achieved, and under what conditions.
- Divide participants into groups of three or four, each group taking one of the changes from worksheet box 1. Ask the groups to use worksheet box 2 to analyse the situation.

Language feedback

- Classify your observation notes (see page 7).
- Acknowledge accurate and appropriate language in the left hand section of your observation sheet (see page 7).
- Pick out classes of error and work on these with participants. See page 9 for techniques of correction and extending language range.
- Present new language which is needed (see page 9).
- Ask participants to write new and corrected language in their personal language files under the headings *Describing change* and *Other language notes*. These are for use during the *Transfer* stage and to keep for future reference.

Transfer

- Ask groups to use their worksheet, personal language file and presentation preparation sheet to present the topic they have discussed, outlining the conditions needed to achieve the desired result and using their diagrams for illustration.

R E M A R K S

If you know the group, you may be aware of a question involving change which is of general interest to them. If so, you can take this case as the example for demonstration purposes.

At stage 4 participants may take it in turns to present different aspects of the case.

O N E - T O - O N E

1 Follow the same procedure, omitting pair or group work and using the worksheet as a framework for discussion with your course participant.
2 Record your conversation on audio-cassette for you and your course participant to analyse later.

13 Aims and objectives

LEVEL   Upper intermediate to advanced   TIME   45 minutes

SUGGESTED LANGUAGE FOCUS

Stating objectives   When making your observation notes, listen in particular for language of aims and objectives which participants:
a) express well.
b) express inaccurately.
c) need to learn in order to communicate their ideas.

PREPARATION

A copy of the worksheet and personal language file for each participant.
A copy of the presentation preparation sheet for each participant.
A copy of the observation sheets for yourself.

Initial task

In stages 1 and 2, help with language to facilitate the task where necessary.

- Divide participants into two or more groups and tell them that you have £100,000 to invest in a new project.
- Ask each group to decide on a project which would be worth your investment.
- Ask each group to give their project a name and to write it in box 1 of their worksheet.

Communicative task

During this stage monitor the discussions and make language notes on the observation sheet (see page 86).

- Ask each group to agree on the aim of the project and to write it in box 2 of the worksheet. Ask the groups to brainstorm ways of achieving their aim and to write them in box 3 of the worksheet.
- Ask them then to prioritise ways of achieving these aims as high, medium and low priority. Set a time limit of 10 to 15 minutes.

Language feedback

- Classify your observation notes (see page 7).
- Acknowledge accurate and appropriate language in the left hand section of your observation sheet (see page 7).
- Pick out classes of error and work on these with participants. See page 9 for techniques of correction and extending language range.
- Present new language which is needed (see page 9).

- Ask participants to write new and corrected language in their personal language files under the headings *Stating objectives* and *Other language notes*. These are for use during the *Transfer* stage and to keep for future reference.

Transfer

- Ask participants to use their worksheet and personal language file, and the presentation preparation sheet, to prepare a presentation stating what the project is, its aims and how they intend to achieve them.
- Ask each participant in the group to present part of the project.

REMARKS

Develop the theme by asking participants how they set aims and objectives in their own work.

ONE-TO-ONE

The activity above is designed for a group. With an individual use the framework in the worksheet to help your participant make a presentation about a past, current or future project.

14 The workplace

L E V E L   Elementary to advanced   **T I M E**   45 minutes

SUGGESTED LANGUAGE FOCUS

Location and position   When making your observation notes, listen in particular for language of location and position which participants:
a) express well.
b) express inaccurately.
c) need to learn in order to communicate their ideas.

PREPARATION

A copy of the worksheet and personal language file for each participant.
A copy of the observation sheets for yourself.

Initial task

In stages 1 and 2, help with language to facilitate the task where necessary.

- Ask participants to draw in box 1 of the worksheet a sketch plan of their work environment – office, shop floor etc. – indicating their own workplace and labelling any adjacent departments, and using arrows to indicate the flow of work.

Communicative task

During this stage monitor the discussions and make language notes on the observation sheet (see page 86).

- Divide participants into pairs. Ask one of each pair to interview the other to find out his or her opinion of the strengths and weaknesses of the present layout, making notes in box 2 of the worksheet.
- Ask them to exchange roles and repeat the task.

Language feedback

- Classify your observation notes (see page 7).
- Acknowledge accurate and appropriate language in the left hand section of your observation sheet (see page 7).
- Pick out classes of error and work on these with participants. See page 9 for techniques of correction and extending language range.
- Present new language which is needed (see page 9).
- Ask participants to write new and corrected language in their personal language files under the headings *Location and position* and *Other language notes*. These are for use during the *Transfer* stage and to keep for future reference.

Transfer

- Ask participants to use their worksheet box 3 and personal language file to prepare justifications for their partner's workplace staying the same, or suggestions for change. Ask participants to present the information in boxes 2 and 3 to the others.

R E M A R K S

For discussion, look out for cross-cultural differences in workplace organisation.

O N E - T O - O N E

Ask participants to complete the worksheet for themselves, and to prepare their own justifications and suggestions, or invent their own ideal workplace.

15 Products and services

L E V E L   Elementary to advanced   T I M E   45 minutes

S U G G E S T E D   L A N G U A G E   F O C U S

Describing products and services   When making your observation notes, listen in particular for language describing products and services which participants:
a) express well.
b) express inaccurately.
c) need to learn in order to communicate their ideas.

P R E P A R A T I O N

A copy of the worksheet and personal language file for each participant.
A copy of the presentation preparation sheet for each participant.
A copy of the observation sheets for yourself.

1 | STAGE ONE | Initial task

In stages 1 and 2, help with language to facilitate the task where necessary.

- Ask participants to describe, in one sentence, a product or service they are involved with. Ask them to write this sentence in box 1 of the worksheet.
- Ask participants to fill in box 2 of the worksheet, giving unique aspects of this product or service (they may not need all the headings).

2 | STAGE TWO | Communicative task

During this stage monitor the discussions and make language notes on the observation sheet (see page 86).

- Ask participants to exchange information in pairs.
- Ask each participant to pick one aspect from box 2 which is of direct concern to them in their work, and to explain this briefly to the group.

3 | STAGE THREE | Language feedback

- Classify your observation notes (see page 7).
- Acknowledge accurate and appropriate language in the left hand section of your observation sheet (see page 7).
- Pick out classes of error and work on these with participants. See page 9 for techniques of correction and extending language range.
- Present new language which is needed (see page 9).
- Ask participants to write new and corrected language in their personal language files under the headings *Describing products and services* and *Other language notes*. These are for use during the *Transfer* stage and to keep for future reference.

Transfer

- Ask participants to use box 3 of the worksheet to describe changes in the product or service from the past to the present, and likely changes in the future. Ask participants to use their worksheet and personal language file to prepare a short presentation on this product or service.

R E M A R K S

If any participants are not directly concerned with a product or service in their work, ask them to regard their own job as a service within the organisation. Alternatively, ask them to pick a consumer product which they are familiar with.

O N E - T O - O N E

1 Follow the same procedure, omitting pair or group work and using the worksheet as a framework for discussion with your course participant.
2 Record your conversation on audio-cassette for you and your course participant to analyse later.

16 Health and safety

L E V E L   Lower intermediate to advanced   T I M E   45 minutes

S U G G E S T E D   L A N G U A G E   F O C U S

Rules and regulations   When making your observation notes, listen in particular for language of rules and regulations which participants:
a) express well.
b) express inaccurately.
c) need to learn in order to communicate their ideas.

P R E P A R A T I O N

A copy of the worksheet and personal language file for each participant.
A copy of the observation sheets for yourself.

Initial task

S T A G E
O N E   1

In stages 1 and 2, help with language to facilitate the task where necessary.

- Ask participants to fill in the grids in boxes 1 and 2 of the worksheet (one for health and one for safety), with examples from their own place of work.

STAGE
TWO

Communicative task

During this stage monitor the discussions and make language notes on the observation sheet (see page 86).

- Ask participants to explain their worksheets to a partner.
- Discuss with the whole group to see if there are any common concerns, and how different organisations deal with different types of risk.

STAGE
THREE

Language feedback

- Classify your observation notes (see page 7).
- Acknowledge accurate and appropriate language in the left hand section of your observation sheet (see page 7).
- Pick out classes of error and work on these with participants. See page 9 for techniques of correction and extending language range.
- Present new language which is needed (see page 9).
- Ask participants to write new and corrected language in their personal language files under the headings *Rules and regulations* and *Other language notes*. These are for use during the *Transfer* stage and to keep for future reference.

STAGE
FOUR

Transfer

- Ask participants to use their worksheet and personal language file to write: a) a five point health and safety plan for their workplace b) five short health or safety notices to be displayed in appropriate locations in their workplace.
- Ask participants to present and explain these items to the group.

R E M A R K S

Many buildings have health and safety notices which can help in describing local conditions. Before using the unit you might like to note the location and content of notices in your premises.

O N E - T O - O N E

1 Follow the same procedure, omitting pair or group work and using the worksheet as a framework for discussion with your course participant.
2 Record your conversation on audio-cassette for you and your course participant to analyse later.

17 What do managers do?

LEVEL Elementary to advanced   TIME 45 minutes

SUGGESTED LANGUAGE FOCUS

Job responsibilities   When making your observation notes, listen in particular for
language of job responsibilities which participants:
a) express well.
b) express inaccurately.
c) need to learn in order to communicate their ideas.

PREPARATION

A copy of the worksheet and personal language file for each participant.
A copy of the observation sheets for yourself.

Initial task

STAGE

ONE 1

In stages 1 and 2, help with language to facilitate the task where necessary.

● Write, at the top of the board, the question: What do managers do?
● Explain that this means: What do **all** managers do, whatever their job?
● Divide participants into small groups and ask them to fill in box 1 of their worksheet with
  words which answer this question.
● Ask the groups to feed these words back to you. Write them at random on the board.

43

2 STAGE TWO — Communicative task

During this stage monitor the discussions and make language notes on the observation sheet (see page 86).

- Ask the groups to work together again to classify the words on the board under headings of their own choice using box 2. See *Remarks* for examples.
- Ask a representative of each group to explain and justify the headings they have chosen.

3 STAGE THREE — Language feedback

- Classify your observation notes (see page 7).
- Acknowledge accurate and appropriate language in the left hand section of your observation sheet (see page 7).
- Pick out classes of error and work on these with participants. See page 9 for techniques of correction and extending language range.
- Present new language which is needed (see page 9).
- Ask participants to write new and corrected language in their personal language files under the headings *Job responsibilities* and *Other language notes*. These are for use during the *Transfer* stage and to keep for future reference.

4 STAGE FOUR — Transfer

- Ask participants to use their worksheet and personal language file to choose from the list something they do in their own job, and explain to the group how they do it.

REMARKS

The above activity is designed to produce a list of verbs, so it can be used with participants at elementary level. For example: *delegate, motivate, instruct, inform, communicate*. With more advanced participants you can rephrase the question as 'What are the roles of a manager?', and this could produce a list of abstract nouns such as: *leadership, responsibility* etc.

It is likely that the answers to the question 'What do managers do?' could be classified under the following headings, which correspond to the sections of this book: *The business world, The organisation, Doing the job, Working with people, Self-management.*

However, other headings could be suggested, for example: Managing people, Managing space, Managing resources, Managing time.

ONE-TO-ONE

1 Follow the same procedure, omitting pair or group work and using the worksheet as a framework for discussion with your course participant.
2 Record your conversation on audio-cassette for you and your course participant to analyse later.

Develop the *Transfer* section to cover several of your participant's job responsibilities in greater depth.

18 Demands, choices and constraints

L E V E L Upper intermediate to advanced   **T I M E** 45 minutes

S U G G E S T E D L A N G U A G E F O C U S

Expressing demands, choices and constraints When making your observation
notes, listen in particular for language expressing demands, choices and constraints which
participants:
a) express well.
b) express inaccurately.
c) need to learn in order to communicate their ideas.

P R E P A R A T I O N

A copy of the worksheet and personal language file for each participant.
A copy of the observation sheets for yourself.

Initial task

In stages 1 and 2, help with language to facilitate the task where necessary.

- Ask participants to prepare a short list of:

    a) things they must do in their job (demands)
    b) things they can choose about in their job (choices)
    c) things which limit them at work (constraints).

- Ask them to list these under the headings a), b) and c) in the diagram in box 1 of the
  worksheet.

Communicative task

*During this stage monitor the discussions and make language notes on the observation sheet
(see page 86).*

- Ask participants to explain their diagrams to a partner.
- Ask participants to tell you some of the items they have under each heading and make
  lists on the board of the demands, choices and constraints they mention.
- Ask participants to use the items in these columns to make complete sentences
  expressing their own demands, choices and constraints at work.

STAGE THREE — Language feedback

- Classify your observation notes (see page 7).
- Acknowledge accurate and appropriate language in the left hand section of your observation sheet (see page 7).
- Pick out classes of error and work on these with participants. See page 9 for techniques of correction and extending language range.
- Present new language which is needed (see page 9).
- Ask participants to write new and corrected language in their personal language files under the headings *Expressing demands, choices and constraints* and *Other language notes*. These are for use during the *Transfer* stage and to keep for future reference.

STAGE FOUR — Transfer

- Ask participants to use their worksheet and personal language file to fill in the table in box 2, indicating the origin of the demands, choices and constraints they have identified.
- Ask participants to explain these to the group.

REMARKS

For background information see Rosemary Stewart's *Choices for the Manager* (see bibliography).
This unit lends itself to modal verb practice.

ONE-TO-ONE

1 Follow the same procedure, omitting pair or group work and using the worksheet as a framework for discussion with your course participant.
2 Record your conversation for you and your course participant to analyse later.

19 Quality

LEVEL Intermediate to advanced   **TIME** 1 hour

SUGGESTED LANGUAGE FOCUS

Explaining problems and solutions   When making your observation notes, listen in particular for language explaining problems and solutions which participants:
a) express well.
b) express inaccurately.
c) need to learn in order to communicate their ideas.

PREPARATION

A copy of the worksheet and personal language file for each participant.
A copy of the observation sheets for yourself.

Initial task

In stages 1 and 2, help with language to facilitate the task where necessary.

● Ask participants to fill in the first part of the worksheet, giving ways in which their work contributes to quality in their department or organisation, and how that contribution to quality is measured.

Communicative task

During this stage monitor the discussions and make language notes on the observation sheet (see page 86).

● Ask participants to explain their notes to a partner, then to pick one aspect of their contribution to quality and explain it to the group.

Language feedback

● Classify your observation notes (see page 7).
● Acknowledge accurate and appropriate language in the left hand section of your observation sheet (see page 7).
● Pick out classes of error and work on these with participants. See page 9 for techniques of correction and extending language range.
● Present new language which is needed (see page 9).
● Ask participants to write new and corrected language in their personal language files under the headings *Explaining problems and solutions* and *Other language notes*. These are for use during the *Transfer* stage and to keep for future reference.

Transfer

Ask participants to use their worksheet and personal language file to fill in the second part of the worksheet, identifying a specific quality problem at work (past or present), and using the questions to form the background to a short case study which they present to the group.

REMARKS

You can develop stage 4 into a group discussion on approaches to quality. The following questions may be useful prompts:

How do you set standards?	How do you improve quality?
How do you achieve standards?	How do you communicate and consult?
How do you measure performance?	How do you determine responsibility?

ONE-TO-ONE

1 Follow the same procedure, omitting pair or group work and using the worksheet as a framework for discussion with your course participant.

2 Record your conversation for you and your course participant to analyse later.

20 Systems

L E V E L   Elementary to advanced   T I M E   1 hour

S U G G E S T E D   L A N G U A G E   F O C U S

Sequencing   When making your observation notes, listen in particular for language of sequencing which participants:
a) express well.
b) express inaccurately.
c) need to learn in order to communicate their ideas.

P R E P A R A T I O N

A copy of the worksheet and personal language file for each participant.
A copy of the observation sheets for yourself.

Initial task

In stages 1 and 2, help with language to facilitate the task where necessary.

- Ask participants to use box 1 of the worksheet to note down some of the systems they use at work and the purpose of each system. Then ask them to choose one, if possible one which they themselves have introduced or are responsible for. Ask them to write down in box 2 all the steps of this system from beginning to end.

Communicative task

During this stage monitor the discussions and make language notes on the observation sheet (see page 86).

- Ask participants to work in pairs and explain their chosen system. Ask them to explain:
  a) what the system is for.
  b) how it works.
  c) its strengths and weaknesses.
- Ask the pairs to report briefly to the group on their discussions then ask the group as a whole to agree on some basic rules for making any system work.

3 STAGE THREE   Language feedback

- Classify your observation notes (see page 7).
- Acknowledge accurate and appropriate language in the left hand section of your observation sheet (see page 7).
- Pick out classes of error and work on these with participants. See page 9 for techniques of correction and extending language range.
- Present new language which is needed (see page 9).

- Ask participants to write new and corrected language in their personal language files under the headings *Sequencing* and *Other language notes*. These are for use during the **Transfer** stage and to keep for future reference.

Transfer

- Ask participants to use their worksheet and personal language file to explain another system from their list in box 1.

R E M A R K S

If participants need prompting at stage 1 feed in some examples relevant to individuals in the group. For example, secretaries have in-tray, post, diary, etc. Sales people have enquiries, response, follow-up, etc. Finance people have reporting systems. Marketing people have research and planning systems. You can find outlines of relevant systems in *The Manager's Handbook* (see bibliography). In the discussion at the end of stage 2 the following themes may be useful prompts.

Clarity: how clear is the system?
Simplicity: how simple is it?
User-friendliness: is it user-friendly?
Achievability: does it achieve the intended result?
Monitoring: how is it monitored?
Feedback: how is feedback given?
Information: what is the role of information?
Communication: how is communication achieved?

O N E - T O - O N E

This unit is particularly useful for one-to-one as it allows detailed discussion of a variety of aspects of the participant's job.

1 Follow the same procedure, omitting pair or group work and using the worksheet as a framework for discussion with your course participant.
2 Record your conversation on audio-cassette for you and your course participant to analyse later.

21 Production processes

L E V E L   Intermediate to advanced   T I M E   1 hour

S U G G E S T E D   L A N G U A G E   F O C U S

Describing processes   When making your observation notes, listen in particular for language describing processes which participants:
a) express well.
b) express inaccurately.
c) need to learn in order to communicate their ideas.

P R E P A R A T I O N

A copy of the worksheet and personal language file for each participant.
A copy of the observation sheets for yourself.
A copy of the presentation preparation sheet for each participant.

Initial task

In stages 1 and 2, help with language to facilitate the task where necessary.

• Ask the group to brainstorm products which are made industrially and put these on the board. Choose one (on the basis of its appropriacy, interest, humour etc.) which participants are **not** directly concerned with themselves, and ask them to work in sub-groups to fill in box 1 of the worksheet, deciding what they will need in order to make the product.

Communicative task

During this stage monitor the discussions and make language notes on the observation sheet (see page 86).

• Ask the groups to prepare a production process flowchart for the product, using box 2 of the worksheet, and transferring the final version to a flipchart.
• Ask each group to present their process, each member of the group explaining a different part of it. Vote on the best process, or a combination.

Language feedback

• Classify your observation notes (see page 7).
• Acknowledge accurate and appropriate language in the left hand section of your observation sheet (see page 7).
• Pick out classes of error and work on these with participants. See page 9 for techniques of correction and extending language range.
• Present new language which is needed (see page 9).

50

- Ask participants to write new and corrected language in their personal language files under the headings *Describing processes* and *Other language notes*. These are for use during the *Transfer* stage and to keep for future reference.

Transfer

- Ask participants to use their worksheet and personal language file to prepare a similar presentation for a production process they are familiar with and to present it to the group.

R E M A R K S

At stage 1 you, or the group, can choose the product. A variation would be for each group to work on a different product.

This unit provides an ideal opportunity for teaching passive forms.

O N E - T O - O N E

Follow the same procedure, working together to prepare a presentation which your participant gives.

22 Meetings

L E V E L   Lower intermediate to advanced   T I M E   1 hour

S U G G E S T E D   L A N G U A G E   F O C U S

Stating aims and procedures   When making your observation notes, listen in particular for language stating aims and procedures which participants:
a) express well.
b) express inaccurately.
c) need to learn in order to communicate their ideas.

P R E P A R A T I O N

A copy of the worksheet and personal language file for each participant.
A copy of the observation sheets for yourself.

Initial task

In stages 1 and 2, help with language to facilitate the task where necessary.

- Ask participants to tell you the different reasons why meetings are held, and write them on the board. Ask participants to classify these reasons into different types of meeting, to pick the types of meeting which they take part in themselves, and to fill in the details in box 1 of the worksheet.

2 | STAGE | TWO Communicative task

During this stage monitor the discussions and make language notes on the observation sheet (see page 86).

- Ask participants to exchange information on the content of box 1. Then ask them to pick one meeting from their list and write it at the top of box 2, indicating which of the listed items applies to that meeting. Participants again exchange information. Then ask the whole group to suggest actions which are essential to ensure successful meetings. Write these on the board.

3 | STAGE | THREE Language feedback

- Classify your observation notes (see page 7).
- Acknowledge accurate and appropriate language in the left hand section of your observation sheet (see page 7).
- Pick out classes of error and work on these with participants. See page 9 for techniques of correction and extending language range.
- Present new language which is needed (see page 9).
- Ask participants to write new and corrected language in their personal language files under the headings *Stating aims and procedures* and *Other language notes*. These are for use during the *Transfer* stage and to keep for future reference.

4 | STAGE | FOUR Transfer

- Ask participants to use their worksheet and personal language file to make suggestions for the improvement of another of their meetings in box 1.

R E M A R K S

See p. 53 for a useful checklist at stage 1.
At stage 2, the usual cycle includes:

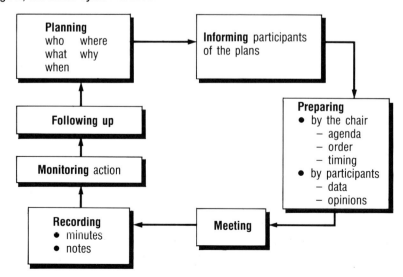

Checklist:

information meetings
planning meetings
discussion meetings
problem-solving meetings
decision-making meetings
negotiating meetings
delegation meetings
maintaining contacts

O N E - T O - O N E

1 Follow the same procedure, omitting pair or group work and using the worksheet as a framework for discussion with your course participant.
2 Record your conversation on audio-cassette for you and your course participant to analyse later.

23 Participating in meetings

L E V E L   Advanced   T I M E   1 hour

S U G G E S T E D   L A N G U A G E   F O C U S

Describing behaviour   When making your observation notes, listen in particular for language describing behaviour which participants:
a) express well.
b) express inaccurately.
c) need to learn in order to communicate their ideas.

P R E P A R A T I O N

A copy of the worksheet and personal language file for each participant.
A copy of the observation sheets for yourself.
In this unit do not hand out the participants' worksheets until after the initial brainstorm.
It is useful to have a flipchart for stages 2 and 4 to free the board for feedback in stage 3.

Initial task	

In stages 1 and 2, help with language to facilitate the task where necessary.

● Ask the group to brainstorm the things people do in meetings which help or hinder the process of the meeting. Write these on the board under the headings:

Speaking behaviour   Body language
Listening behaviour   Observance of procedures

Hand out the worksheets and ask participants to think of a meeting they attend, and to tick the types of behaviour which people display in that meeting, giving examples.

Communicative task

During this stage monitor the discussions and make language notes on the observation sheet (see page 86).

- Ask participants to discuss their worksheets in pairs. As a group discuss the most common forms of behaviour which hinder meetings. List these on a flip chart for use at stage 4.

Language feedback

- Classify your observation notes (see page 7).
- Acknowledge accurate and appropriate language in the left hand section of your observation sheet (see page 7).
- Pick out classes of error and work on these with participants. See page 9 for techniques of correction and extending language range.
- Present new language which is needed (see page 9).
- Ask participants to write new and corrected language in their personal language files under the headings *Describing behaviour* and *Other language notes*. These are for use during the *Transfer* stage and to keep for future reference.

Transfer

- Ask participants to use their worksheet and personal language file to suggest ways of dealing with behaviour mentioned in stage 2 and produce a checklist of guidelines for chairing meetings. Work in small groups or as a whole group.

REMARKS

A checklist for the role of the chair is:

achieve aims
guide the discussion
control timing
eliminate digressions
listen and observe
summarise each discussion briefly
resolve conflict
involve participants

ONE-TO-ONE

Treat the brainstorm and group activities as discussion with your course participant. You will be able to treat the issues in more depth than the group context allows.

24 Problem solving

L E V E L   Advanced   T I M E   1½ hours

S U G G E S T E D   L A N G U A G E   F O C U S

Hypothesizing, comparing alternatives   When making your observation notes, listen in particular for language of hypothesizing and comparing alternatives which participants:
a) express well.
b) express inaccurately.
c) need to learn in order to communicate their ideas.

P R E P A R A T I O N

Two copies of the worksheet and personal language file for each participant.
A copy of the observation sheets for yourself.
You will need a problem to be solved, in the form of a theme, article, case study, etc.
Make two copies of the worksheet for each course participant, so that they have one to use in the *Transfer* stage.

Initial task

In stages 1 and 2, help with language to facilitate the task where necessary.

- Ask participants to tell you what methods they use at work to solve problems. For example, do they use informal meetings or structured meetings? What structure is used? Write these on the board.
- Now present the problem to be discussed, and ask participants to agree on a definition which they write in box 1 of the worksheet.
- Ask the group to brainstorm associated problems, and to express each of these as a question requiring a solution, beginning: 'How can we . . .?'. For example if the problem is pollution, the associated questions might be:

How can we reduce exhaust emissions?
How can we clean up rivers?
How can we dispose of nuclear waste?
How can we reduce the effects of pollution?

- Ask participants to write these questions in box 2.

Communicative task

During this stage monitor the discussions and make language notes on the observation sheet (see page 86).

- Divide into sub-groups and ask them to brainstorm all the solutions they can think of. Ask them also to include all the craziest solutions they can think of. Note them in box 3 of the worksheet.
- Now ask groups to look at each proposed solution in turn and answer the question, 'Why might this solution not work?', in as many ways as they can, using box 4. Ask them to eliminate all but the best solutions, leaving perhaps two or three viable possibilities. They use box 5 of the worksheet.
- Groups now present their solutions and individuals vote on their preferred choice.

STAGE THREE — Language feedback

- Classify your observation notes (see page 7).
- Acknowledge accurate and appropriate language in the left hand section of your observation sheet (see page 7).
- Pick out classes of error from the second section of your observation sheet and work on these with participants. See page 9 for techniques of correction and extending language range.
- Present new language which is needed (see page 9).
- Ask participants to write new and corrected language in their personal language files under the headings *Hypothesizing*, *comparing alternatives* and *Other language notes*. These are for use during the *Transfer* stage and to keep for future reference

STAGE FOUR — Transfer

- Ask participants to identify a current problem of their own at work and to use their worksheet and personal language file to outline possible solutions, reasons why they might or might not work and recommend a course of action.

REMARKS

This problem solving framework has 5 steps:

1 Definition of the problem
2 Alternative expressions of the problem
3 Generating ideas
4 Eliminating ideas
5 Deciding action

You may find that in stage 1 of this unit your group produces a similar framework or an equally valid one, in which case you can choose to use this for the exercise (and note it for future use).

ONE-TO-ONE

In order to generate as many ideas as possible in stage 1, prepare some ideas yourself to prompt reflection.

Alternatively, focus on the problem-solving process itself as a theme for discussion, taking the one illustrated in the worksheet as a springboard.

56

25 Graphs and Charts

L E V E L   Elementary to advanced   T I M E   1 hour

S U G G E S T E D   L A N G U A G E   F O C U S

Presenting visual information   When making your observation notes, listen in particular for language of presenting visual information which participants:
a) express well.
b) express inaccurately.
c) need to learn in order to communicate their ideas.

P R E P A R A T I O N

A copy of the worksheet and personal language file for each participant.
A copy of the observation sheets for yourself.

Initial task

In stages 1 and 2, help with language to facilitate the task where necessary.

● Ask participants what types of graph and chart they use at work. Ask them to draw these on the board.
  In the whole group, brainstorm themes which can be illustrated using a graph or chart. Put these on the board at random.

Communicative task

● *During this stage monitor the discussions and make language notes on the observation sheet (see page 86).*

● Divide into sub-groups and ask each group to choose a theme from the board and an appropriate way of representing it visually, and to prepare it for presentation to the others, using worksheet box 1.
● Each group appoints a spokesperson who presents their diagram using the whiteboard.

Language feedback

● Classify your observation notes (see page 7).
● Acknowledge accurate and appropriate language in the left hand section of your observation sheet (see page 7).
● Pick out classes of error and work on these with participants. See page 9 for techniques of correction and extending language range.
● Present new language which is needed (see page 9).
● Ask participants to write new and corrected language in their personal language files under the headings *Presenting visual information* and *Other language notes*. These are for use during the *Transfer* stage, and to keep for future reference.

Ask participants to use their worksheet and personal language file to prepare a short presentation using graphs or charts relating to their work. Box 2 of the worksheet is provided for this.

REMARKS

Language needed will vary according to the type of graph or chart used:

1 Line graph 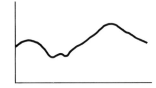 Volume, time, trends, vertical and horizontal movements, rates of change. Past, present and future forms can be used.

2 Pie chart 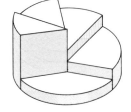 Proportions, relative sizes, percentages, comparisons, contrasts.

3 Bar chart 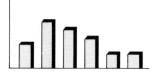 A bar chart is a type of histogram. Comparisons, trends, volume, time. Comparisons of past, present and future.

4 Histogram 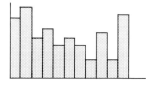 A histogram looks like a bar chart but can be used for planning purposes, because bars or sections of bars can be moved from one position to another to illustrate different scenarios. Certain types of wall planner are histograms.
Conditionals, hypothesis, time.

5 Scattergram  Distribution, norms, distance, quantity, comparisons.

Actual examples from books or from the press often contain a large amount of information in a small space. This can make them good subjects for discussion with a more advanced group. Advance preparation is useful as initial impressions are sometimes misleading.

ONE-TO-ONE

1 Follow the same procedure, omitting pair or group work and using the worksheet as a framework for discussion with your course participant.
2 Record your conversation on audio-cassette for you and your course participant to analyse later.

26 Controlling and monitoring

L E V E L   Upper intermediate to advanced   T I M E   1 hour

S U G G E S T E D   L A N G U A G E   F O C U S

Cause and effect   When making your observation notes, listen in particular for
language of cause and effect which participants:
a) express well.
b) express inaccurately.
c) need to learn in order to communicate their ideas.

P R E P A R A T I O N

A copy of the worksheet and personal language file for each participant.
A copy of the observation sheets for yourself.

Initial task

STAGE
O N E
1

In stages 1 and 2, help with language to facilitate the task where necessary.

● Ask each participant to write in box 1 some of the objectives which they have at work.
● Ask participants to choose one of these for discussion and underline it. This should be an objective which other participants can easily understand.
● Ask participants to write in box 2 what action is needed to achieve the objective.
● Ask participants to fill in box 3 explaining the method of monitoring the action.
● Ask participants to write in box 4 the standards against which achievement of the objective is measured (e.g. time, money, specification etc.).

Communicative task

STAGE
T W O
2

During this stage monitor the discussions and make language notes on the observation sheet (see page 86).

● In pairs, participants explain boxes 1 to 4 to each other, asking questions where necessary.
● Ask participants to fill in box 5, showing how they can adjust the action, the standards or the objective itself if the process is not producing the desired result.
● Pairs exchange information on box 5 then briefly report to the group.

3 STAGE THREE — Language feedback

- Classify your observation notes (see page 7).
- Acknowledge accurate and appropriate language in the left hand section of your observation sheet (see page 7).
- Pick out classes of error and work on these with participants. See page 9 for techniques of correction and extending language range.
- Present new language which is needed (see page 9).
- Ask participants to write new and corrected language in their personal language files under the headings *Cause and effect* and *Other language notes*. These are for use during the *Transfer* stage and to keep for future reference.

4 STAGE FOUR — Transfer

- Ask participants to choose another of the objectives in box 1 and to use their worksheet and personal language file to present a control cycle to the group which is appropriate to this objective.

R E M A R K S

Because controlling and monitoring is a cyclical activity (action – monitoring – adjustment – action) there is scope for practising the language of cause and effect with concrete examples from individuals' own work. Objectives in stage 1 could be: human objectives, economic or financial objectives, time objectives, space objectives, quality objectives, quantity objectives.

O N E - T O - O N E

Work on an objective chosen by your course participant, who fills in the boxes as you ask the questions, then explains the answers to you. Record the conversation on audio-cassette as you may not have time to fill in the observation sheet during the discussion.

27 Planning

L E V E L   Lower intermediate to advanced   T I M E   1½ hours

S U G G E S T E D   L A N G U A G E   F O C U S

Explaining logistics   When making your observation notes, listen in particular for language explaining logistics which participants:
a) express well.
b) express inaccurately.
c) need to learn in order to communicate their ideas.

P R E P A R A T I O N

A copy of the worksheet and personal language file for each participant.
A copy of the observation sheets for yourself.
A flipchart and coloured pens.

Initial task

In stages 1 and 2, help with language to facilitate the task where necessary.

- Ask participants to write down in box 1 of the worksheet some aspects of their work which involve planning. These could be related to: human resources, time, budgets, materials, equipment, training etc.
- Ask each participant to choose one of their examples from box 1, and to fill in box 2 to illustrate the level of planning (corporate, project or task) and the details involved.

Communicative task

During this stage monitor the discussions and make language notes on the observation sheet (see page 86).

- Ask participants to exchange information in pairs using box 3 of the worksheet to draw a skeleton diagram of the planning process they use.
- Ask participants to transfer the diagram in box 3 to a flipchart and present it.

STAGE THREE — Language feedback

- Classify your observation notes (see page 7).
- Acknowledge accurate and appropriate language in the left hand section of your observation sheet (see page 7).
- Pick out classes of error and work on these with participants. See page 9 for techniques of correction and extending language range.
- Present new language which is needed (see page 9).
- Ask participants to write new and corrected language in their personal language files under the headings *Explaining logistics* and *Other language notes*. These are for use during the *Transfer* stage and to keep for future reference.

STAGE FOUR — Transfer

- *Either* ask participants to use their worksheet and personal language file to prepare a presentation on another aspect of their work which involves planning.
- *Or* ask the group to hold a meeting to prepare a plan for an activity or event which they will be involved in together.

REMARKS

Planning techniques vary according to the object of the plan so you may find interesting comparisons in the diagrams in box 3.

Factors for use in group discussion at the end of stage 2 include:
How much flexibility does the plan have?
How do you monitor execution of the plan?
How is the plan updated?
How do you estimate requirements for:
time, equipment, costs, people, location, space, movements?

ONE-TO-ONE

1 Follow the same procedure, omitting pair or group work and using the worksheet as a framework for discussion with your course participant.
2 Record your conversation on audio-cassette for you and your course participant to analyse later.

WORKING WITH PEOPLE

28 Job advertisements

L E V E L   Upper intermediate to advanced   T I M E   45 minutes

S U G G E S T E D   L A N G U A G E   F O C U S

Job descriptions   When making your observation notes, listen in particular for language
of job descriptions which participants:
a) express well.
b) express inaccurately.
c) need to learn in order to communicate their ideas.

P R E P A R A T I O N

A copy of the two worksheets and personal language file for each participant.
A copy of the observation sheets for yourself.
You will need about six job advertisements from the press. Distribute them to
participants.

Initial task

STAGE
O N E   **1**

In stages 1 and 2, help with language to facilitate the task where necessary.

●   Distribute the advertisements to the group. Ask participants to note significant aspects of
each job in box 1 of the worksheet.

Communicative task

During this stage monitor the discussions and make language notes on the observation sheet (see page 86).

- As a group, compare notes. Check understanding and make sure that no relevant information has been missed.
- As a group discuss how well-designed the advertisements are, and how they might be different in participants' own countries.
- Ask participants to fill in box 2 of the worksheet, giving details of their own job.
- In pairs, using the headings in box 1 of the worksheet ask participants to interview each other to obtain information in order to write an advertisement for the other person's job in the *Transfer* stage.

Language feedback

- Classify your observation notes (see page 7).
- Acknowledge accurate and appropriate language in the left hand section of your observation sheet (see page 7).
- Pick out classes of error and work on these with participants. See page 9 for techniques of correction and extending language range.
- Present new language which is needed (see page 9).
- Ask participants to write new and corrected language in their personal language files under the headings *Job descriptions* and *Other language notes*. These are for use during the *Transfer* stage and to keep for future reference.

Transfer

- Ask participants to use their worksheet and personal language file to write job advertisements for their partners.
- If working with a group, display the advertisements and ask the group to identify the person whose job is advertised.

R E M A R K S

Style, register and wording of advertisements can be discussed.

O N E - T O - O N E

Ask your participant to write a job advertisement for their own job.

29 Staff selection

LEVEL Elementary to advanced   TIME 45 minutes

SUGGESTED LANGUAGE FOCUS

Narrating past experience   When making your observation notes, listen in particular for language narrating past experience which participants:
a) express well.
b) express inaccurately.
c) need to learn in order to communicate their ideas.

PREPARATION

A copy of the worksheet and personal language file for each participant.
A copy of the observation sheets for yourself.

Initial task

In stages 1 and 2, help with language to facilitate the task where necessary.

● Ask participants to choose the statement in box 1 of the worksheet which best describes how they were selected for their present job.
● Now ask them to fill in box 2 with the stages of the selection process which they experienced.

Communicative task

During this stage monitor the discussions and make language notes on the observation sheet (see page 86).

● Ask participants to exchange information in pairs, noting similarities and differences.
● In the whole group, discuss the different procedures experienced, and their effectiveness.

Language feedback

● Classify your observation notes (see page 7).
● Acknowledge accurate and appropriate language in the left hand section of your observation sheet (see page 7).
● Pick out classes of error and work on these with participants. See page 9 for techniques of correction and extending language range.
● Present new language which is needed (see page 9).
● Ask participants to write new and corrected language in their personal language files under the headings *Narrating past experience* and *Other language notes*. These are for use during the *Transfer* stage and to keep for future reference.

STAGE FOUR — Transfer

- Ask participants to use their worksheet box 3 and personal language file to prepare a plan to recruit a new team member, and to present this to the group.

REMARKS

In the group discussion in stage 2, central questions are:
How do you decide whether the person could do the job?
How do you decide whether the person would do the job?
How do you decide whether the person would fit in with the team?

ONE-TO-ONE

1 Follow the same procedure, omitting pair or group work and using the worksheet as a framework for discussion with your course participant.
2 Record your conversation on audio-cassette for you and your course participant to analyse later.

In stage 2, you may wish to describe your own experience for a previous job.

30 Communication

LEVEL Elementary to advanced   TIME 45 minutes

SUGGESTED LANGUAGE FOCUS

Communication systems   When making your observation notes, listen in particular for language of communication systems which participants:
a) express well.
b) express inaccurately.
c) need to learn in order to communicate their ideas.

PREPARATION

A copy of the worksheet and personal language file for each participant.
A copy of the observation sheets for yourself.

STAGE ONE — Initial task

In stages 1 and 2, help with language to facilitate the task where necessary.

- In box 1 of the worksheet, ask participants to note means of communication they use at work.
- With the whole group, brainstorm reasons for communicating at work and note these on the board.

- Ask participants to note in box 2 who they communicate with at work, giving names where possible. They should also add the reasons for communicating with each one.

Communicative task

During this stage monitor the discussions and make language notes on the observation sheet (see page 86).

- In pairs, ask participants to explain their diagrams to each other, with those listening asking questions to determine whether communication is effective or whether there are breakdowns.
- As a group, discuss breakdowns which have been pinpointed, and recommend action, or give guidelines for good communication.

Language feedback

- Classify your observation notes (see page 7).
- Acknowledge accurate and appropriate language in the left hand section of your observation sheet (see page 7).
- Pick out classes of error and work on these with participants. See page 9 for techniques of correction and extending language range.
- Present new language which is needed (see page 9).
- Ask participants to write new and corrected language in their personal language files under the headings *Communication systems* and *Other language notes*. These are for use during the *Transfer* stage and to keep for future reference.

Transfer

- *Either* ask participants to use their worksheet and personal language file to identify a communication problem at work, to present it to the group and to discuss solutions.
- *Or* ask participants to describe any special communication system they use at work.

REMARKS

Means of communication include:
face to face
telephone
fax
letters
memos
meetings
in-trays
electronic mail
video conferencing
notice-boards
pigeon-holes

Reasons for communication include:
giving information
transmitting messages
arranging meetings
maintaining relationships
discussing problems
getting information

In the spider diagram, the lines can be made longer or shorter, or thicker or thinner, to indicate the strength and importance of the relationship.

This unit provides an opportunity to discover the following:

1 Situations where the participant uses the native language or English.
2 Methods of communication most often used.
3 The register appropriate to each type of exchange.
4 Typical content of exchanges.

You can use this information as part of a needs analysis.

ONE-TO-ONE

The activity can be used equally in a one-to-one situation. You can go into some detail and find information which will be useful for building on in further lessons.

The exercise can lead to role plays where you take the part of one of the people your course participant has to speak to. Ask the participant to give you relevant background information based on 1 to 4 above.

31 Appearance, character and behaviour

LEVEL Elementary to advanced   TIME 45 minutes

SUGGESTED LANGUAGE FOCUS

Describing people   When making your observation notes, listen in particular for language describing people which participants:
a) express well.
b) express inaccurately.
c) need to learn in order to communicate their ideas.

PREPARATION

A copy of the worksheet and personal language file for each participant.
A copy of the observation sheets for yourself.

STAGE ONE — **Initial task**

In stages 1 and 2, help with language to facilitate the task where necessary.

- Ask participants to think of a colleague at work and to fill in box 1 of the worksheet with a physical description. Now ask them to fill in box 2 giving details of their character and behaviour in the different situations listed.

Communicative task

During this stage monitor the discussions and make language notes on the observation sheet (see page 86).

- Ask participants to exchange information in pairs. When this has been done ask participants to give you all the expressions they have used to describe people, and write these on the board under the headings Appearance, Character and Behaviour. These notes will serve in stage 3 as a supplement to your observation sheet.

Language feedback

- Classify your observation notes (see page 7).
- Acknowledge accurate and appropriate language in the left hand section of your observation sheet (see page 7).
- Pick out classes of error and work on these with participants. See page 9 for techniques of correction and extending language range.
- Present new language which is needed (see page 9).
- Ask participants to write new and corrected language in their personal language files under the headings *Describing people* and *Other language notes*. These are for use during the *Transfer* stage and to keep for future reference.

Transfer

- *Either* ask participants to use their worksheet and personal language file to give a description of another colleague at work.
- *Or* ask participants to write a description of their ideal colleague, subordinate or boss.

R E M A R K S

You can expand the list of words on the board by writing up synonyms or opposites, using different colours.

In stage 1, box 2 you may need to prompt by asking participants to remember specific events or situations where their colleague exhibited a particular aspect of behaviour.

In stage 1 you may wish to ask participants to describe someone outside their company, or someone who is not known to the group.

O N E - T O - O N E

1 Follow the same procedure, omitting pair or group work and using the worksheet as a framework for discussion with your course participant.
2 Record your conversation on audio-cassette for you and your course participant to analyse later.

32 Working with your boss

L E V E L   Upper intermediate to advanced   T I M E   45 minutes

S U G G E S T E D   L A N G U A G E   F O C U S

Describing values and behaviour   When making your observation notes, listen in particular for language describing values and behaviour which participants:
a) express well.
b) express inaccurately.
c) need to learn in order to communicate their ideas.

P R E P A R A T I O N

A copy of the worksheet and personal language file for each participant.
A copy of the observation sheets for yourself.

Initial task

In stages 1 and 2, help with language to facilitate the task where necessary.

- Ask participants to fill in box 1 of the worksheet with details of their boss or of a boss they have had in a previous job, giving the boss's aims, values, strengths, weaknesses etc.
- Ask participants to indicate on the worksheet whether each item has/had a positive or negative effect on them.

Communicative task

During this stage monitor the discussions and make language notes on the observation sheet (see page 86).

- In pairs participants compare worksheets and explain the reasons for these effects.
- Ask participants to write down, in the second part of the worksheet, three things they try to do in order to maintain a good relationship with their boss.
- Ask each member of the group to choose one item and explain it to the group.

3 | STAGE THREE | Language feedback

- Classify your observation notes (see page 7).
- Acknowledge accurate and appropriate language in the left hand section of your observation sheet (see page 7).
- Pick out classes of error and work on these with participants. See page 9 for techniques of correction and extending language range.
- Present new language which is needed (see page 9).
- Ask participants to write new and corrected language in their personal language files under the headings *Describing values and behaviour* and *Other language notes*. These are for use during the *Transfer* stage and to keep for future reference.

Transfer

S T A G E

F O U R · 4

Ask participants to use their worksheet and personal language file to write notes for a new colleague giving advice on how to get on well with the boss. Participants explain these to the group.

R E M A R K S

At stage 4 look out for use of modals.

O N E - T O - O N E

1 Follow the same procedure, omitting pair or group work and using the worksheet as a framework for discussion with your course participant.
2 Record your conversation on audio-cassette for you and your course participant to analyse later.

33 Motivating people

L E V E L Advanced   T I M E 45 minutes

S U G G E S T E D   L A N G U A G E   F O C U S

Describing attitudes and responses   When making your observation notes, listen in particular for language describing attitudes and responses which participants:
a) express well.
b) express inaccurately.
c) need to learn in order to communicate their ideas.

P R E P A R A T I O N

A copy of the worksheet and personal language file for each participant.
A copy of the observation sheets for yourself.

Initial task

S T A G E

O N E · 1

In stages 1 and 2, help with language to facilitate the task where necessary.

- As a group, brainstorm factors which motivate people to work. Put these on the board.
- Now hand out the worksheet. Ask participants to add in to box 1 any of the items on the board which are not included in the diagram.
- Ask participants to think of an occasion when they felt highly motivated at work, and the reasons for their motivation. Ask them to write these in box 2 of the worksheet, using box 1 for reference.

STAGE TWO — Communicative task

During this stage monitor the discussions and make language notes on the observation sheet (see page 86).

- Ask participants to explain their notes to each other in pairs, and to discuss any similarities and differences. As a group review common factors and discuss any unusual or individual cases. Also discuss any differences between motivating individuals and motivating teams.

STAGE THREE — Language feedback

- Classify your observation notes (see page 7).
- Acknowledge accurate and appropriate language in the left hand section of your observation sheet (see page 7).
- Pick out classes of error and work on these with participants. See page 9 for techniques of correction and extending language range.
- Present new language which is needed (see page 9).
- Ask participants to write new and corrected language in their personal language files under the headings *Describing attitudes and responses* and *Other language notes*. These are for use during the *Transfer* stage and to keep for future reference.

STAGE FOUR — Transfer

- Ask participants to use their worksheet and personal language file to remember an occasion when they were demotivated at work, and to explain the reasons why.

REMARKS

A convenient way of classifying motivators is as follows:
a) Those which come from within a person: e.g. *learning, self-realisation.*
b) Those which are outside the person: e.g. *pay, working conditions, perks, recognition, promotion prospects.*

For background information see *Management and Motivation* (see bibliography) especially chapter 2 (Maslow's theory of human motivation), chapter 7 (Hertzberg's Motivation-Hygiene theory), and chapter 22 (McGregor's The Human Side of Enterprise).

ONE-TO-ONE

You may wish to talk about your own experience of motivation, using examples from your past experience in a previous job.

34 People problems

L E V E L   Advanced   T I M E   1 hour

S U G G E S T E D   L A N G U A G E   F O C U S

Expressing feelings   When making your observation notes, listen in particular for language expressing feelings which participants:
a) express well.
b) express inaccurately.
c) need to learn in order to communicate their ideas.

P R E P A R A T I O N

A copy of the two worksheets and personal language file for each participant.
A copy of the observation sheets for yourself.

Initial task

In stages 1 and 2, help with language to facilitate the task where necessary.

- Ask participants to fill in box 1 of the worksheet, giving three or four examples.

Communicative task

During this stage monitor the discussions and make language notes on the observation sheet (see page 86).

- Ask participants to compare notes, to classify them under the headings in box 2, and to explain these to the group.
- Ask them individually to read the checklist in box 3 and to indicate which of the responses is their natural reaction to each of the four characteristics they described in box 1. Ask them to discuss their answers in pairs.
- Ask the group to discuss appropriate action in the cases individuals have outlined in box 1. Individuals can make notes in box 4.

Language feedback

- Classify your observation notes (see page 7).
- Acknowledge accurate and appropriate language in the left hand section of your observation sheet (see page 7).
- Pick out classes of error and work on these with participants. See page 9 for techniques of correction and extending language range.
- Present new language which is needed (see page 9).
- Ask participants to write new and corrected language in their personal language files under the headings *Expressing feelings* and *Other language notes*. These are for use during the *Transfer* stage and to keep for future reference.

Transfer

- Ask participants to use their worksheet and personal language file to describe a people problem from their recent experience, explaining the behaviour and reactions involved, and how the problem was dealt with.

R E M A R K S

If mutual support, respect and trust are strong in the group, individuals will be more inclined to talk about their feelings. If the climate is weaker, generalisations will be more appropriate. The continuum is:

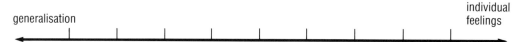

generalisation

individual feelings

and you can control the balance by the way you ask questions. For example, you can ask: 'How do you feel?', in order to get a personal response, or: 'In your experience, how do people react?' to get a generalised response rather than a personal reaction. The response may in fact be the same, but the individual will feel less pressured.

O N E - T O - O N E

Use yourself as the partner. Use this unit once you have built up a climate of trust with your participant. The one-to-one situation allows greater openness.

35 Working in a team

L E V E L Upper intermediate to advanced   T I M E 1 hour

S U G G E S T E D   L A N G U A G E   F O C U S

Describing teams When making your observation notes, listen in particular for language describing teams which participants:
a) express well.
b) express inaccurately.
c) need to learn in order to communicate their ideas.

P R E P A R A T I O N

A copy of the worksheet and personal language file for each participant.
A copy of the observation sheets for yourself.

1
S T A G E
O N E

Initial task

In stages 1 and 2, help with language to facilitate the task where necessary.

- Ask participants to draw a diagram of their team in box 1 using a dot for each person, and lines to show who communicates with whom. Ask them to write a name and job function beside each dot.

    Then ask them to fill in the questionnaire in box 2.

Communicative task

During this stage monitor the discussions and make language notes on the observation sheet (see page 86).

- Ask participants to compare and discuss the information on their worksheets in pairs.
- Ask participants to report briefly back to the group and to discuss how team function and structure are related.

Language feedback

- Classify your observation notes (see page 7).
- Acknowledge accurate and appropriate language in the left hand section of your observation sheet (see page 7).
- Pick out classes of error from the second section of your observation sheet and work on these with participants. See page 9 for techniques of correction and extending language range.
- Present new language which is needed (see page 9).
- Ask participants to write new and corrected language in their personal language files under the headings *Describing teams* and *Other language notes*. These are for use during the *Transfer* stage and to keep for future reference.

Transfer

Ask participants to use their worksheet and personal language file to suggest ways in which they would set about building up a new team.

R E M A R K S

For information on teams and communication within teams, see the books by Charles Handy listed in the bibliography, particularly *Understanding Organisations*, chapter 6 (On the workings of groups).

O N E - T O - O N E

As above for worksheet box 1.

Take the questionnaire point by point discussing where appropriate. Record the discussion on audio-cassette for you and your course participant to analyse later.

Alternatively give your participant the worksheet to complete beforehand.

36 Training

L E V E L   Lower intermediate to advanced   T I M E   1½ hours

S U G G E S T E D   L A N G U A G E   F O C U S

Evaluating needs   When making your observation notes, listen in particular for language of evaluating needs which participants:
a) express well.
b) express inaccurately.
c) need to learn in order to communicate their ideas.

P R E P A R A T I O N

A copy of the two worksheets and personal language file for each participant.
A copy of the observation sheets for yourself.

Initial task

In stages 1 and 2, help with language to facilitate the task where necessary.

* Ask participants to fill in box 1 of the worksheet for the present language training course, or for another course they have recently attended.

Communicative task

During this stage monitor the discussions and make language notes on the observation sheet (see page 86).

* Ask participants to tell the group what they have written. Discuss any points of interest.
* Ask participants to fill in box 2 of the worksheet with details of training they have received at work. Ask them to discuss this in pairs and to comment on the effectiveness or otherwise of this training.
* As a group, discuss participants' different experiences and whether they vary according to company or culture. Discuss also what makes training effective.

Language feedback

* Classify your observation notes (see page 7).
* Acknowledge accurate and appropriate language in the left hand section of your observation sheet (see page 7).
* Pick out classes of error and work on these with participants. See page 9 for techniques of correction and extending language range.
* Present new language which is needed (see page 9).
* Ask participants to write new and corrected language in their personal language files under the headings *Evaluating needs* and *Other language notes*. These are for use during the *Transfer* stage, and to keep for future reference.

Transfer

- *Either* ask participants to use their worksheet and personal language file to draw up and justify a training plan for a newcomer to the company taking over their job.
- *Or* ask participants to make a training plan for their own future. They should use box 3 of the worksheet for this, and present it to the group.

R E M A R K S

Points for group discussion in stage 2 are:

Is training linked to corporate objectives?
Is it planned and budgeted for?
How are training decisions made?
How is training evaluated by the organisation?
How do individuals respond to and evaluate training?

O N E - T O - O N E

1 Follow the same procedure, omitting pair or group work and using the worksheet as a framework for discussion with your course participant.
2 Record your conversation on audio-cassette for you and your course participant to analyse later.

37 Job satisfaction

LEVEL Upper intermediate to advanced   **TIME** 1½ hours

SUGGESTED LANGUAGE FOCUS

Expressing opinions   When making your observation notes, listen in particular for
language of opinions which participants:
a) express well.
b) express inaccurately.
c) need to learn in order to communicate their ideas.

PREPARATION

A copy of the worksheet and personal language file for each participant.
A copy of the observation sheets for yourself.

1 STAGE ONE Initial task

In stages 1 and 2, help with language to facilitate the task where necessary.

- Ask participants how important they think job satisfaction is. Ask them what the
  components (for themselves or their subordinates) of this satisfaction are? Write these on
  the board.

- Ask participants to answer the questionnaire in worksheet box 1, giving reasons or examples for their answers in the space provided.

Communicative task

During this stage monitor the discussions and make language notes on the observation sheet (see page 86).

- In pairs, ask participants to compare and explain their answers to each other.
- As a group, discuss how their answers to the questionnaire reflect the items on the board. Add any new items and rank them in order of importance.

Language feedback

- Classify your observation notes (see page 7).
- Acknowledge accurate and appropriate language in the left hand section of your observation sheet (see page 7).
- Pick out classes of error and work on these with participants. See page 9 for techniques of correction and extending language range.
- Present new language which is needed (see page 9).
- Ask participants to write new and corrected language in their personal language files under the headings *Expressing opinions* and *Other language notes*. These are for use during the *Transfer* stage and to keep for future reference.

Transfer

- *Either* ask participants to use their worksheet and personal language file to prepare and present a short documentary for radio or television entitled 'Job satisfaction in industry', to include live interviews and summaries.
- *Or* ask participants to carry out a survey using the questionnaire, and present their findings.

REMARKS

In stage 1 questions to ask are:

What helps to make your job satisfying?
Do other people play a part in this satisfaction?
Do your working conditions affect job satisfaction?
Is your pay important to your satisfaction?
When did you last feel particularly satisfied about some aspect of your job?

In stage 2 participants can add items mentioned in stage 1 to the questionnaire.

ONE-TO-ONE

Concentrate on discussing items in the questionnaire.

38 Self-assessment

L E V E L   Upper intermediate to advanced   T I M E   45 minutes

S U G G E S T E D   L A N G U A G E   F O C U S

Expressing likes and dislikes   When making your observation notes, listen in particular for language of likes and dislikes which participants:
a) express well.
b) express inaccurately.
c) need to learn in order to communicate their ideas.

P R E P A R A T I O N

A copy of the worksheet and personal language file for each participant.
A copy of the observation sheets for yourself.

1 STAGE ONE   Initial task

In stages 1 and 2, help with language to facilitate the task where necessary.

● Ask participants to fill in box 1 of the worksheet with three things they like, and three things they dislike about their present job.

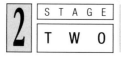

2 STAGE TWO   Communicative task

During this stage monitor the discussions and make language notes on the observation sheet (see page 86).

● Ask participants to exchange information in pairs.
● Ask participants to rate themselves individually on the scales given in worksheet box 2 (they can add other dimensions if they wish).
● Ask participants to exchange information in pairs noticing whether any items in box 2 correspond with items in box 1.
● Ask the group to feed back to you the main points they have discussed. Put these on the board. Ask whether participants have regular appraisal interviews at work which give them an opportunity to discuss job performance and satisfaction.

3 STAGE THREE   Language feedback

● Classify your observation notes (see page 7).
● Acknowledge accurate and appropriate language in the left hand section of your observation sheet (see page 7).
● Pick out classes of error and work on these with participants. See page 9 for techniques of correction and extending language range.
● Present new language which is needed (see page 9).

- Ask participants to write new and corrected language in their personal language files under the headings *Expressing likes and dislikes* and *Other language notes*. These are for use during the *Transfer* stage and to keep for future reference.

Transfer

- Ask participants to use their worksheet and personal language file to prepare for an appraisal interview with their boss next week, and to fill in worksheet box 3 in preparation for it.
- In pairs participants role play the appraisal interview taking turns to play the roles of manager and employee.

R E M A R K S

Instead of the role play in the *Transfer* stage participants may prefer to discuss their own experience of appraisal interviews, and the system of appraisal within their organisation.

O N E - T O - O N E

Concentrate on the participant's own assessment, using the worksheet as a basis. In the *Transfer* stage, take the part of the boss.

39 Time management

L E V E L   Elementary to advanced   T I M E   45 minutes

S U G G E S T E D   L A N G U A G E   F O C U S

Expressions of time and proportion   When making your observation notes, listen in particular for language of time and proportion which participants:
a) express well.
b) express inaccurately.
c) need to learn in order to communicate their ideas.

P R E P A R A T I O N

A copy of the worksheet and personal language file for each participant.
A copy of the observation sheets for yourself.

Initial task

In stages 1 and 2, help with language to facilitate the task where necessary.

- Ask participants how many hours there are in a week.
- Draw a circle on the board which represents the 168 hours in a week. Ask participants to use the first circle on their worksheet to show the relative proportion of time which a) is committed to their work, b) is available for their own use, c) is spent sleeping.

STAGE TWO Communicative task

During this stage monitor the discussions and make language notes on the observation sheet (see page 86).

- Ask pairs to compare how time is spent, noting differences.
- Ask participants to use the second circle on the worksheet to indicate the relative amount of time they spend at work on the following:
  1) breaks and lunch
  2) time which is organised for them
  3) time which they organise themselves.
- Ask pairs to compare and discuss their diagrams.
- Ask each participant to put their second pie chart on the board. Discuss common points and differences in the group.

STAGE THREE Language feedback

- Classify your observation notes (see page 7).
- Acknowledge accurate and appropriate language in the left hand section of your observation sheet (see page 7).
- Pick out classes of error and work on these with participants. See page 9 for techniques of correction and extending language range.
- Present new language which is needed (see page 9).
- Ask participants to write new and corrected language in their personal language files under the headings *Expressions of time and proportion* and *Other language notes*. These are for use during the *Transfer* stage and to keep for future reference.

STAGE FOUR Transfer

- Ask participants to use their worksheet and personal language file to fill in box 3 of the worksheet with three ways in which they could improve their use of time at work, and to present these to the group.

REMARKS

From a time management point of view, time can be divided into *discretionary* time (which you can use as you wish) and *committed* time (which is already spoken for), and the pie charts should bring out this distinction.

If you encourage participants to give as much detail as possible, you will discover their core or compulsory tasks, and to what extent they can organise their own time.

The information you get about their work will help in choosing themes for further activities.

ONE-TO-ONE

Ask your participant to fill in the first pie chart and explain; follow the same procedure for the second pie chart; find out whether your participant would like to make any changes to use of time and ask him or her to explain and illustrate using the charts.

40 Stress management

L E V E L   Upper intermediate to advanced   T I M E   45 minutes

S U G G E S T E D   L A N G U A G E   F O C U S

Physical and emotional states   When making your observation notes, listen in particular for language of physical and emotional states which participants:

a) express well.

b) express inaccurately.

c) need to learn in order to communicate their ideas.

P R E P A R A T I O N

A copy of the worksheet and personal language file for each participant.

A copy of the observation sheets for yourself.

Initial task

In stages 1 and 2, help with language to facilitate the task where necessary.

- Ask participants to note in box 1 of the worksheet sources of stress which they have observed at work, coming from individuals themselves, relations between people, or organisational pressures.
- Ask for some examples under each heading, and put them up on the board.
- Now ask participants to tick the reactions in box 2 which they have observed in others as a result of stress.

Communicative task

During this stage monitor the discussions and make language notes on the observation sheet (see page 86).

- Ask participants to discuss their notes with a partner, explaining when they observed the reactions they have noted.
- Ask participants to tell the group of cases of people under stress at work.

Language feedback

- Classify your observation notes (see page 7).
- Acknowledge accurate and appropriate language in the left hand section of your observation sheet (see page 7).
- Pick out classes of error and work on these with participants. See page 9 for techniques of correction and extending language range.
- Present new language which is needed (see page 9).
- Ask participants to write new and corrected language in their personal language files under the headings *Physical and emotional states* and *Other language notes*. These are for use during the *Transfer* stage and to keep for future reference.

STAGE

FOUR Transfer

- Ask participants to fill in box 3 of the worksheet with their own methods of coping with stress, whether emotional, physical or mental.
- Ask participants to use their worksheet and personal language file to present these ideas for group discussion.

REMARKS

If the climate and culture of the group allow, you may wish to write in (or add verbally) additional items for worksheet box 3: e.g. drugs, alcohol, etc.

ONE - TO - ONE

1 Follow the same procedure, omitting pair or group work and using the worksheet as a framework for discussion with your course participant.
2 Record your conversation on audio-cassette for you and your course participant to analyse later.

41 Career development

LEVEL Upper intermediate to advanced   TIME 1 hour

SUGGESTED LANGUAGE FOCUS

Past, present and future When making your observation notes, listen in particular for language of rules and regulations which participants:
a) express well.
b) express inaccurately.
c) need to learn in order to communicate their ideas.

PREPARATION

A copy of the two worksheets and personal language file for each participant.
A copy of the observation sheets for yourself.

STAGE

ONE Initial task

In stages 1 and 2, help with language to facilitate the task where necessary.

- Ask participants to fill in box 1 of the worksheet as a personal assessment of their present position at work, making notes on their own existing strengths and weaknesses, the opportunities open to them, and the threats to the status quo.

Communicative task

STAGE TWO 2

During this stage monitor the discussions and make language notes on the observation sheet (see page 86).

- Ask participants to discuss their notes in pairs.
- Now ask participants to write in box 2 the major influences on them at critical moments in their career development to date, and to discuss in pairs.
- As a group, discuss the different parts played, in career development, by planning, choice, and circumstances outside the individual's control.

Language feedback

STAGE THREE 3

- Classify your observation notes (see page 7).
- Acknowledge accurate and appropriate language in the left hand section of your observation sheet (see page 7).
- Pick out classes of error and work on these with participants. See page 9 for techniques of correction and extending language range.
- Present new language which is needed (see page 9).
- Ask participants to write new and corrected language in their personal language files under the headings *Past, present and future* and *Other language notes*. These are for use during the *Transfer* stage and to keep for future reference.

Transfer

STAGE FOUR 4

- Ask participants to use their worksheet and personal language file to fill in box 3 of the worksheet, forming a personal action plan for the future, and to present this to the group.

R E M A R K S

The three sections of the unit correspond to present, past and future career development and provide an opportunity to practise appropriate verb forms.

O N E - T O - O N E

1 Follow the same procedure, omitting pair or group work and using the worksheet as a framework for discussion with your course participant.
2 Record your conversation on audio-cassette for you and your course participant to analyse later.

Initial observation notes

Language focus of this exercise: _____

Good use of language	Language to be corrected	Possible correct version

Classified observation notes

Language focus of this exercise: _____

Good use of language	Language to be corrected	Possible correct version

Other language items: _____

Good use of language	Language to be corrected	Possible correct version

Personal language file

Theme: _____

notes

Other language notes

Presentation preparation sheet

		Language reminders
1	**Introduction of speaker**	
2	**Theme of presentation**	
3	**Main points of presentation**	
4	**Presentation**	
	Part one	
	Part two	
	Part three	
	Part four	
5	**Conclusion**	
6	**Questions**	

What do you do?

1 Main tasks in my job

1

2

3

4

5

6

7

8

2 Classification

1 The business world

2 The organisation

3 Doing the job

4 Working with people

5 Self-management

The market

1 **Product or service:** _____
Sold to: ☐ Individual consumers ☐ Business

2

State of the market	Reason
☐ stable	
☐ fluctuating	
☐ growing	
☐ shrinking	
☐ new	
☐ established	
☐ changing	
☐ other	

3 Factors which influence customers in the market

2 The future of business

Objectives for the future of business	Action needed to achieve these objectives
1	
2	
3	

Cultural differences in business

1

	How did you notice this?	How did it affect your work?
Appointments		
Business cards		
Business correspondence		
Decision making		
Hours of work		
Negotiating		
Telephoning		
Business entertainment		
Business meetings		
Dress		

2 Note down three ways in which a foreign business visitor might find your country's business conventions different from theirs.

1

2

3

4 Cultural differences in society

1 Country: _____

	How was it different?	What had you expected?
Alcohol		
Body language		
Leisure		
Cars		
Education		
Food		
Tipping		
Animals		
Advertising		
Quality of life		

2 Note down three things which might be new to a foreign visitor to your country.

1

2

3

Demographic trends

1   **Country:** _____

	Rising	Falling	Notes
Birth rate			
Average age of population			
Proportion of male employees			
Proportion of female employees			
Proportion of full-time employees			
Proportion of part-time employees			
Average age of employees			
Proportion of native employees			
Proportion of immigrant employees			
Average level of education			
Other			

2

Main demographic factors affecting the workforce at present in my organisation:	Main demographic factors which will affect the workforce in future in my organisation:

3   Main demographic factors affecting the market for our products and services in the future

product or service

6 The natural environment

Resources and raw materials

1	needed from the environment	effects on the environment

Geographical location of the organisation

2	needed from the environment	effects on the environment

Process and co-ordination

3	needed from the environment	effects on the environment

Products and services

4	needed from the environment	effects on the environment

Long-term considerations

5	

STEP analysis

1   My organisation

Sociological factors	Technological factors
1	1
2	2
Economic factors	**Political/legal factors**
1	1
2	2

2   My partner's organisation

Sociological factors	Technological factors
1	1
2	2
Economic factors	**Political/legal factors**
1	1
2	2

8 Company structure

1 **Structure of company or department**

2 Tick the boxes which you consider to be the main causes of your company's present structure
- [ ] the company's history
- [ ] the company's ownership
- [ ] the size of the company
- [ ] the products or services of the company
- [ ] technology used by the company
- [ ] the company's values and objectives
- [ ] the environment
- [ ] the people in the company

Company culture

Answer the following questions about the atmosphere at your place of work, giving examples where possible.

Question	Yes	No	Example
Do people dress formally?			
Does everyone have lunch in the same place?			
Is there a high turnover of staff?			
Do people use first names?			
Are people consulted about policies affecting them?			
Is there a good relationship with management?			
Do people socialise out of work?			
Are decisions made quickly?			
Are people forward-looking?			
Are people aware of the market for your product or service?			
Is everyone involved in the quality process?			
Do people work as a team?			
Do people keep strict times?			
Do people make jokes?			

10 SWOT analysis

1 My organisation

	Strengths	Weaknesses
internal		
	Opportunities	Threats
external		

2 My partner's organisation

	Strengths	Weaknesses
internal		
	Opportunities	Threats
external		

1

Normal working hours	
Days worked	
Holidays	
Public holidays	
Sick leave	
Maternity/Paternity leave	
Bonus payments	
Perks	
Other	

12 Managing change

1 | An aspect of my work I would like to change

2 |

Factors which will obstruct achievement of the desired result

people:　　*equipment:*　　*money:*　　*time:*　　*space:*

| desired result of change |

Factors which will help achievement of the desired result

people:　　*equipment:*　　*money:*　　*time:*　　*space:*

Aims and objectives

1   **Project name:** _____

2   **The aim of the project**

3

Ways of achieving the aims	Priority		
	High	Medium	Low

14 The workplace

1 Plan of workplace

2

	Strengths	Weaknesses
Environment factors: *light* *noise* *heat* *space* *privacy*		
Equipment factors: *machinery* *furnishings* *decor*		
Communication factors: *internal* *external*		
Workflow factors: *inwards* *outwards*		

3 Justifications for present layout

Suggestions for change

Products and services

1 **Product/Service:** _____
Description

2 **Unique aspects of this product/service**

Quality aspects:

Performance aspects:

Design aspects:

Specification aspects:

3 **Changes in the product/service: past, present and future**

16 Health and safety

Health

Give examples of potential health hazards at your place of work, and corresponding methods of prevention.

1

Cause of hazard	Type of hazard	Possible effects	Method of prevention
People			
Premises			
Equipment			
Processes			
Materials			
Products			
Natural phenomena			

Safety

Give examples of accident risks at your place of work, and corresponding safety procedures.

2

Cause of accident	Type of accident	Risk to people	Risk to equipment	Safety procedure
People				
Premises				
Equipment				
Processes				
Materials				
Products				
Natural phenomena				

What do managers do?

17

WORKSHEET

1 | What do managers do?

2 | Classification

© Longman Group UK Ltd 1992

18 Demands, choices and constraints

1

a) **Demands**
1
2
3

c) **Constraints**
1
2
3

b) **Choices**
1
2
3

2	Source of demands, choices or constraints					
	The organisation	Boss	Colleagues	Self	Outside world	Other
Demands:						
1						
2						
3						
Choices:						
1						
2						
3						
Constraints:						
1						
2						
3						

Quality

1

Ways in which my work contributes to quality in my department or organisation		How is quality measured?
Technical ways:		
Administrative ways:		
Intellectual ways:		
Creative ways:		
Interpersonal ways:		
Other ways:		

2

Quality problem	
What exactly is the problem?	
Where is it found?	
When does it occur?	
Why does it occur?	
How does it occur?	
Who is affected by the problem?	
Who can help to find a solution?	

20 Systems

1 Systems I use at work

System	Purpose

2 Chosen system: _____

Steps

1

2

3

4

5

6

7

8

9

10

11

12

Production processes

1

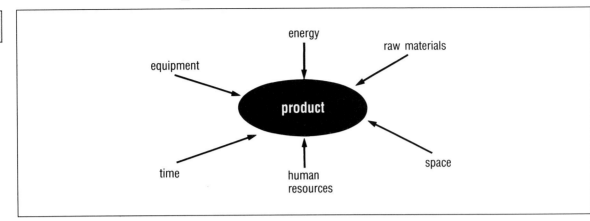

2 **Flowchart of process**

22 Meetings

1 Meetings in my work

Type				
Aim				
Frequency				
Participants				
Formal or informal				
My own role				

2 Chosen type of meeting: _____

- [ ] Advance notice is given
- [ ] All participants prepare in advance
- [ ] An agenda is drawn up
- [ ] The meeting is chaired
- [ ] Strict timing is observed
- [ ] Minutes are taken
- [ ] Minutes are circulated
- [ ] Decisions are followed up

Participating in meetings

Meeting: _____

	Yes?	Example
Speaking behaviour Speaking too much Speaking too little Speaking concisely Waffling Repeating things Interrupting Presenting information clearly Using humour		
Listening behaviour Paying attention Not paying attention Misunderstanding Checking understanding Reflective listening Ignoring		
Body language Fidgeting Doodling Showing attention Showing impatience Showing interest Showing emotion Eye contact		
Observance of procedures Being well prepared Being unprepared Being aware of time Being unaware of time Sticking to the agenda Digressing		

24 Problem solving

1 Definition of problem: _____

2 **Alternative expressions of problem**

How can we . . .
How can we . . .
How can we . . .
How can we . . .
How can we . . .

3 **Possible solutions**

Crazy solutions

4

_____ might not work because . . .

_____ might not work because . . .

_____ might not work because . . .

5 **Best solutions**

Graphs and charts

1 | **Chosen theme:** _____

2 | **Graph or chart relating to my own work**

26 Controlling and monitoring

1 **Objectives at work**

a)
b)
c)
d)

2 **Action needed to achieve the objective**

3 **Monitoring method**

4 **Standards**

5 **Adjustment**

Action	Standards	Objective

Planning

1 | **Aspects of my work which involve planning**

2 | Planning for _____ is:
- ☐ corporate planning
- ☐ project planning
- ☐ task planning within a project

It involves planning for:

	Details
Time	
Equipment	
Costs	
People	
Location	
Space	

3 | **Skeleton diagram of the planning process used**

28

Job advertisements

Ad	1	2	3	4	5	6
Type of job						
Qualifications/ Experience						
Working conditions						
Salary						
Responsibilities						
Skills needed						
Personality needed						

Company	
Job Title	
Responsibilities	
Qualifications and experience needed	
Working conditions	
Reporting relationships	
Personality needed	
Skills needed	
Age range	
Other	

W O R K S H E E T

29 Staff selection

1 How I was selected for my job

- ☐ I responded to a specific job advertisement
- ☐ I wrote to the company
- ☐ I was headhunted
- ☐ I was transferred from another department
- ☐ I was promoted
- ☐ I was recruited at university
- ☐ I was a trainee at the company
- ☐ I had a temporary job at the company
- ☐ I took a job in my family's firm
- ☐ Other

2 Stages of the selection process in my case

3 How I would recruit a new team member

Communication

1 | Means of communication I use at work

2 | People I communicate with for my work

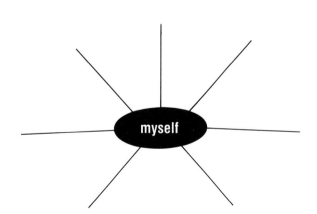

31 Appearance, character, behaviour

1 Appearance

Build	
Style	
Height	
Hair	
Colour of eyes	
Age	
Other	

2 Character and behaviour

On the telephone	
In meetings	
In personal relationships	
Under pressure	
With management	
With subordinates	
In informal situations	
In formal situations	

Working with your boss

1

My boss	Effect on me	
	positive	negative
My boss's aims		
My boss's values		
Pressures on my boss		
My boss's strengths		
My boss's weaknesses		
My boss's idiosyncrasies		

2

Methods of maintaining a good relationship with my boss
1
2
3

33 Motivating people

1

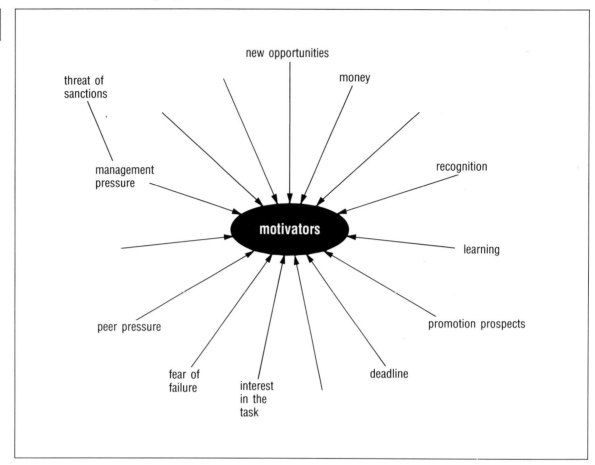

new opportunities

money

threat of
sanctions

management
pressure

recognition

motivators

learning

peer pressure

promotion prospects

fear of
failure

interest
in the
task

deadline

2

I felt highly motivated when: _____

Reasons:

1

2

3

4

People problems

1 | **A difficult person for me is someone who . . .**

1. _____

2. _____

3. _____

4. _____

2 | **Difficult people**

Values

Attitudes

Body language

Speech

3

The behaviour in box 1 makes me feel:	Characteristics			
	1	2	3	4
Frustrated				
Angry				
Sad				
Disgusted				
Irritated				
Afraid				
Guilty				
Resentful				
Jealous				
Envious				
Anxious				
Impatient				
Hurt				
Vulnerable				
Contemptuous				
Embarrassed				

4 To improve the situations in box 1, I need to act in the following ways:

1. _____

2. _____

3. _____

4. _____

Working in a team

1 Structure of my team

2 Questionnaire

Questionnaire	Yes	No
Team identity		
Is your team the right size?		
Does it have the right mix of people?		
Is the workload distributed fairly?		
Is its work recognised by other teams?		
Does it have an effective hierarchy?		
Team objectives		
Does the team have both long-term and short-term objectives?		
Does it have a clear set of standards?		
Does everyone accept both the objectives and the standards?		
Does the team believe it will be successful?		
Does it make the best use of resources?		
Team dynamics		
Do team members know each other well?		
Do they work well together?		
Is there enough communication?		
Do they enjoy themselves?		
Is there an effective system for praise and criticism of team members?		

 **Training**

Course title: _____
How were your needs identified?
What objectives were set?
How was the method of training decided?
How will the training be evaluated?
What arrangements did you have to make in order to attend the course?

Types of training I have received	Examples
Induction	
Job-specific training	
Communication skills training	
Interpersonal skills training	
Management training	
Other	

Training plan for: _____

Needs	Training objectives	Method of training	Method of evaluation

37 Job satisfaction

		Yes	No	Notes
1	Are all your skills being used in your present job?			
2	Is your job recognised as significant?			
3	Do you have responsibility?			
4	Do you have autonomy?			
5	Do you get feedback on your work?			
6	Does your salary reflect the importance of your job?			
7	Does your job present challenges?			
8	Do you have promotion prospects?			
9	Is the atmosphere pleasant?			
10	Are working conditions satisfactory?			
11	Do you receive adequate training?			
12	Do you receive additional rewards like perks and bonuses?			

Self-assessment

1

	Likes	Dislikes
1		
2		
3		

2 Put a cross on each line to indicate your opinion of yourself

prefer to work alone ◄──────────────────► prefer to work in a team

like taking risks ◄──────────────────► plan to avoid risks

like variety ◄──────────────────► like routine

like to work in one place ◄──────────────────► like travelling

prefer to talk ◄──────────────────► prefer to listen

prefer to manage ◄──────────────────► prefer to be managed

like pressure ◄──────────────────► dislike pressure

prefer to think ◄──────────────────► prefer to act

take a long-term view ◄──────────────────► take a short-term view

feel own skills are being used ◄──────────────────► feel own skills are being wasted

◄──────────────────►

◄──────────────────►

◄──────────────────►

3 **Self-assessment**

1. Aspects of my job which I find fulfilling:

2. Aspects of my job which I find demotivating:

3. Personal strengths:

4. Personal weaknesses:

5. Suggestions for further development:

39 Time management

1 **My time**

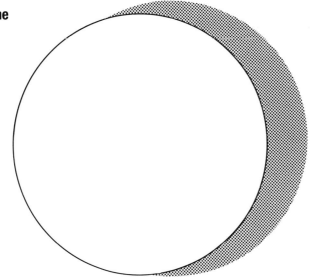

2 **My time at work**

3	Three ways in which I could improve my use of time at work
	1
	2
	3

Stress management

1 | Sources of stress at work

1 Sources within individuals:

2 Interpersonal sources:

3 Organisational sources:

2 | Reactions to stress at work

	Yes/No		Yes/No
Anger		Insomnia	
Irritability		Tiredness	
Depression		Headaches	
Anxiety		Greater energy	
Change of mood		Greater enthusiasm	
Withdrawal		High work output	
Forgetfulness		Alertness	
Loss of concentration		Enjoyment of pressure	
Confusion			
Loss of creativity			

3 | Methods of coping with stress

- Emotional methods

- Physical methods

- Mental methods

WORKSHEET 41

Career development

	The present			
	Strength	Weakness	Opportunity	Threat
Self-knowledge: – likes – dislikes – values – job aims				
Knowledge: – of the job – of the organisation – of the industry – of the business world				
Relationships: – with boss – with colleagues – with others				
Abilities: – job specific – management – communication				

1

2

The past		
Influences	**Planned**	**Unplanned**
People		
Place		
Circumstances		

3

The future: personal action plan	
Short-term aims:	**Long-term aims:**
1	1
2	2
3	3

Requirements	Short-term	Long-term
Training		
Finance		
Support		

BIBLIOGRAPHY

The following books are recommended for background reading.

SECTION ONE: THE BUSINESS WORLD

Peter Drucker 1989 *The New Realities.* Mandarin
Examines political and economic issues over the coming years, and their implications for business and society.

John Harvey-Jones 1988 *Making it Happen.* Fontana
Reflections on his own career, including interesting chapters on the role of the board of directors and the company chairman.

SECTION TWO: THE ORGANISATION

Charles B Handy 1990 *Inside Organisations.* BBC
Twenty-one ideas to prompt managers to think about their own organisation and their role in it.

Charles B Handy 1976 *Understanding Organisations.* Penguin
An examination of organisational structure and culture, and the role of people in organisations.

Peters and Waterman 1982 *In Search of Excellence.* Harper and Row
An examination of key factors leading to success in a number of American companies.

D S Pugh 1989 *Writers on Organisations.* Penguin
Summaries of the findings of influential researchers into organisational behaviour.

John Mole 1988 *Management Mole.* Corgi
An amusing account of everyday life in large organisations, with some serious lessons for managers.

SECTION THREE: DOING THE JOB

Peter Drucker 1988 *Effective Executive.* Heinemann Professional
The elements of effectiveness in business, including two chapters on decision-making.

Peter Stemp 1988 *Are You Managing?* Industrial Society Press
Checklists for key management tasks.

Stephanie Winston 1983 *The Organised Executive.* Kogan Page
Frameworks and checklists for organising tasks at work, including project planning.

Rosemary Stewart 1982 *Choices for the Manager.* McGraw-Hill

Arthur Young 1986 *The Manager's Handbook.* Sphere
Concise two-page summaries of a wide range of business tasks. The checklists are a useful input to lesson plans. Also handy for reading up key job tasks in preparation for one-to-one courses.

SECTION FOUR: WORKING WITH PEOPLE

E N Chapman 1989 *Improving Relations at Work.* Kogan Page
A workbook for developing human relations skills.

Fisher and Ury 1987 *Getting to Yes.* Arrow
The classic textbook on negotiation.

Thomas A Harris 1973 *I'm OK You're OK.* Pan
An introduction to Transactional Analysis

Victor H. Vroom and Edward L. Deci 1989 *Management and Motivation.* Penguin
A summary of research carried out into motivation at work.

NB: The Manager's Handbook (see above) and The Personal Management Handbook
(see below) contain useful sections on working with people.

SECTION FIVE: SELF-MANAGEMENT

J Mulligan 1988 *The Personal Management Handbook.* Sphere
Practical exercises for personal development.

Roger Black 1987 *Getting Things Done.* Michael Joseph
More practical exercises for personal development.

John Adair 1988 *Effective Time Management.* Pan
A guide to the effective use of time: "How to save time and spend it wisely".

Gael Lindenfield 1987 *Assert Yourself.* Thorsons
An introduction to assertiveness skills.

Jane Cranwell-Ward 1990 *Thriving on Stress.* Routledge
A workbook which aims to develop a positive view of stress.